Stories of **GHOSTS**
FROM THE PETAVATTHU

One of the books of the Khuddaka Nikaya.
A translation into English from the Sinhala translation
by
Ven. Kiribathgoda Gnānānanda Thera.

A Mahamegha Publication

Stories of GHOSTS

FROM THE PETAVATTHU

Ven. Kiribathgoda Gnānānanda Thera

© All Rights Reserved

ISBN: 978-955-687-016-9

1st Print: Nawam Full Moon Poyaday - 2556 B.E. (Feb. 2013)

2nd Edition: April 2018

Computer Typesetting by

Buddha Meditation Centre- Greater Toronto

Markham, Ontario, Canada L6C 1P2

Telephone: 905-927-7117

www.mahamevnawa.ca

Published by

Mahamegha Publishers

Waduwawa, Yatigaloluwa, Polgahawela, Sri Lanka.

Telephone: +94 37 2053300 | +94 76 8255703

mahameghapublishers@gmail.com

Printed by

Tharanjee Prints

506, Highlevel Road, Nawinna, Maharagama, Sri Lanka.

Telephone: +94 11 2801308 / +94 11 5555265

Dedication

As there are lotuses that rise clear above the water and seek the nourishing beam of the sun, there are beings who seek the wisdom of the Supreme Buddha's Dhamma.

May they achieve the ultimate bliss of Nibbāna.

About this Book

Most of us are able to see beings who have been reborn in the human realm and many of the beings born in the animal realm. But it is very rare to have the opportunity to witness for ourselves the suffering experienced by those beings born in the ghost realm. Our great teacher, the Supreme Buddha, had an excellent knowledge and vision to be able to see these beings as well as the action that led to the suffering that they experience. In this book, Stories of Ghosts, we can learn about many kinds of ghosts and the bad actions they did to be reborn in the ghost world.

Some ghosts had done bad actions with their body, such as the former deer hunter who, in the ghost world, was torn to shreds by dogs day after day. Other ghosts had done bad things with their speech, such as the ghost who had the mouth of a pig. Even our mental actions can lead to rebirth as a ghost. In this book you will learn about the ghost who held many wrong views and because of that was eventually going to be born in hell for many eons. Some ghosts experience suffering because of not doing things such as practicing generosity.

Because it is not easy to see the results of our own actions immediately, the information in this book will help us to make wise choices about what we do and don't do.

Contents

Lokavabodha Sutta

"Bhikkhus, the world has been fully understood by the Tathāgata; the Tathāgata is released from the world.

Bhikkhus, the origin of the world has been fully understood by the Tathāgata; the origin of the world has been eradicated by the Tathāgata.

Bhikkhus, the cessation of the world has been fully understood by the Tathāgata; the cessation of the world has been realized by the Tathāgata.

Bhikkhus, the path leading to the cessation of the world has been fully understood by the Tathāgata; the path leading to the cessation of the world has been developed by the Tathāgata.

Bhikkhus, in this world with its devas, māras and brahmās; with its recluses and brahmins, among humankind with its princes and people, whatever is seen, whatever is heard, whatever is smelled, whatever is tasted, whatever is touched, whatever is cognized, whatever is attained, whatever is sought, and whatever is comprehended, all have been fully understood by the Tathāgata.

Thus, the Blessed One is called the Tathāgata.

Bhikkhus, from the night when the Tathāgata awakened to unsurpassed Supreme Enlightenment until the night when the Tathāgata passes away into Nibbāna, with nothing remaining, whatever the Tathāgata speaks, utters, and explains, all that is just so, and not otherwise.

Thus, the Blessed One is called the Tathāgata.

Bhikkhus, as the Tathāgata says, so the Tathāgata does. As the Tathāgata does, so the Tathāgata says. In this way, as the Tathāgata says, so the Tathāgata does. As the Tathāgata does, so the Tathāgata says.

Thus, the Blessed One is called the Tathāgata.

Bhikkhus, in this world, with its devas, māras, and brahmās, with its recluses and brahmins, among humankind with its princes and people, the Tathāgata is the conqueror, unvanquished, all-seer, wielding power.

Thus, the Blessed One is called the Tathāgata.

This was said by the Blessed One. So, with regard to this, it was said:

By knowledge of the whole world, the whole world as it truly is, the Blessed One is released from all the world, in all the world the Blessed One is unattached.

The all-conquering heroic sage, freed from every bond is the Blessed One; the Blessed One has reached that perfect peace, Nibbāna which is free from fear.

Rid of taints, the Blessed One is enlightened, free from suffering, and free from doubts; has destroyed all kamma, and is released by the full destruction of clinging.

Our Supreme Buddha, our Blessed One, is a lion, unsurpassed; for in the world together with its devas, the Blessed One set the Brahma-wheel in motion.

Thus those devas and human beings, gone for refuge to the Supreme Buddha, on meeting the Blessed One, pay homage— the Greatest One, free from diffidence.

i. Tamed, the Blessed One is unsurpassed in taming others.
ii. Calmed, the Blessed One is unsurpassed in calming others.
iii. Freed, the Blessed One is unsurpassed in freeing others.
iv. Crossed over, the Blessed One is unsurpassed in helping others to cross over.

Thus, they pay due homage to the Blessed One, the Greatest One free from diffidence, by saying:

"In the world together with its devas, there is no other equalling you, our Supreme Buddha."

Khuddaka Nikāya
Itivuttaka 112

All have I overcome, all-knowing am I;
with regard to all things, unattached.
Having renounced all,
and released in the end of craving;
having fully comprehended on my own,
whom shall I call 'my teacher'?

The gift of Dhamma surpasses all gifts;
the taste of Dhamma, all tastes;
delight in Dhamma, all delights.
One who has destroyed craving,
vanquishes all suffering.

Gautama Supreme Buddha
Dhammapada, verses 353-354

Introduction

Meritorious Sons, Daughters, and Devotees,

We are very fortunate to learn about the knowledges of the Supreme Buddha. Our great teacher, the Supreme Buddha, had an extraordinary knowledge to see past lives of beings. In the Bhayaberava Sutta the Buddha tells us how he gained the knowledge to see his own past lives:

> When my mind was concentrated, purified, bright, clear, free from defilements, open, soft, steady, and unshakeable, I directed my mind to the knowledge of recollecting my past lives. I recollected my various past lives, that is, one birth, two... five, ten... fifty, a hundred, a thousand, a hundred thousand, many eons of the cycle of formation and destruction of this earth. In one life I had such a name, belonged to such a clan, had such an appearance. Such was my food, such my experience of pleasure and pain, such the end of my life. Passing away from that life, I was reborn in another place. There too I had such a name, belonged to such a clan, had such an appearance. Such was my food, such my experience of pleasure and pain, such the end of my life. Passing away from that state, I was reborn here. I remembered my different past lives in every detail.

> This was the first knowledge I attained in the first watch of the night. My ignorance was destroyed, knowledge arose, darkness was destroyed, light arose which happens in one who is mindful, passionate, and firm.

Next the Supreme Buddha gained the knowledge to see how other beings travel in this cycle of samsara, one life to another, because of their good and bad actions.

> When my mind was concentrated, purified, bright, clear, free from defilements, open, soft, steady, and unshakeable, I directed it to gain the knowledge of the passing away and rebirth of beings. With my divine eye which is purified and surpassing the human eye, I saw beings passing away and re-appearing, and I discovered how they are inferior and superior, beautiful and ugly, fortunate and unfortunate in accordance with their kamma: beings who committed bad actions by body, speech and mind, who insulted enlightened ones, held wrong views and did bad deeds because of it, with the break-up of their body, after death, have been reborn in a bad destination, the lower realms, in hell. But those beings who committed good deeds with body, speech, and mind, who did not insult enlightened ones, who held right views and did good deeds because of it, with the break-up of the body, after death, have been reborn in the good destinations, in the heavenly world. Therefore with the use of my divine eye, which is purified and surpassing the human eye, I saw beings passing away and reborn, and I discovered how they are inferior and superior, beautiful and ugly, fortunate and unfortunate in accordance with their kamma.

The Supreme Buddha is the knower of all worlds. He knows the qualities of all the worlds and the way beings are born in these different worlds as he explains in the Maha Sihanada Sutta:

Sariputta, there are five type of beings. What are the

five? Hell beings, animals, ghosts, human beings and gods.

I understand hell, and the path and way leading to hell. And I also understand how people who will be born in hell, on the breaking up of the body, after death, reappear in a state of misery, in an unhappy destination, miserable, in hell.

I understand the animal world, and the path and way leading to the animal world. And I also understand how one who has entered this path will, on the breaking up of the body, after death, be reborn as an animal.

I understand the realm of ghosts, and the path and way leading to the realm of ghosts. And I also understand how one who has entered this path will, on the breaking up of the body, after death, reappear in the realm of ghosts.

I understand human beings, and the path and way leading to the human world. And I also understand how one who has entered this path will, on the breaking up of the body, after death, reappear among human beings.

I understand the gods, and the path and way leading to the world of the gods. And I also understand how one who has entered this path will, on the breaking up of the body, after death, reappear in a happy destination, in the heavenly world.

And most fortunately, Noble Disciples have the opportunity to escape from all worlds by attaining Nibbana. The Supreme Buddha is the only teacher to show the way to Nibbana.

I understand Nibbana, and the path and way leading to Nibbana. I also understand how one who has entered this path will, by realizing it for himself with direct knowledge, here and now enter upon and abide in the liberation of the mind and liberation by wisdom that is taintless with the destruction of the taints.

From this book you are going to learn the actions that lead to the ghost world and how beings are suffering living as ghosts. You will notice that they all lived in the human world like we do now. Here, the Supreme Buddha explains the suffering of the ghost world with a simile:

By investigating a person's mind using my psychic powers I understand how that person behaves. This person having behaved in such a way, on the dissolution of the body, after death, will reappear in the realm of ghosts. Later on, I see that he has reappeared in the realm of ghosts and is experiencing much painful feelings. Suppose there was a tree growing on uneven ground with few leaves creating little shade, and then a man burnt and exhausted by hot weather, tired, dry and thirsty, headed to that tree in hopes of resting in the shade. A wise person then sees the thirsty man who has taken the path towards the tree and realizes that the path that man is on will lead him to a dry tree.

Read these stories very carefully. Think about your own life and how you can apply the lessons these ghosts have learned from their bad behavior in the human world. May these stories help you to develop a fear of doing wrong actions in your precious human life.

May you practice generosity. May you keep the precepts well. May you control your bad thoughts. By practicing

Dhamma, may you escape from rebirth in the ghost world and all bad worlds.

May all of you realize the Four Noble Truths in this Gautama Buddha's Dispensation.

With metta,
Ven. Kiribathgoda Gnānānanda Thera
Mahamevnawa Monastery,
Waduwawa, Yatigal-oluwa, Polgahawela.
Sri Lanka.
2556 Buddhist Years/ 2013

1. The Snake Chapter

1.1 Like a Field

Arahants are like fertile fields. Givers are like the farmers, and what they offer is the seed. The combination of these three will produce a fruit of merit.

The seed, the planting of the seed, and the field are helpful to the givers and their departed relatives. The departed relatives experience happiness from the merit and the givers will receive more merit.

By doing wholesome deeds and sharing the merits that they receive with departed relatives, they are reborn in heaven to enjoy the results of their good deeds.

1.2 Pig's Mouth

Narada Bhante:

Your body is the color of gold and shines in all directions. But your mouth is like a pig's. What have you done in your previous life?

Ghost:

I did nothing wrong with my body, but I said bad things using my mouth. That is why my body is beautiful but my mouth is like a pig's, Narada Bhante.

So Bhante, Now that you can see my body, I strongly encourage you not to do bad things using your mouth, or you will also have the mouth of a pig and suffer like me.

1.3 Stinky Mouth

Narada Bhante:

Your body is as beautiful as an angel and you are floating in the sky. But your mouth is being eaten by worms and is very smelly. What have you done in your previous life?

Ghost:

I was an evil monk and insulted others using bad words. I pretended to be a good monk. I did not control what I said to others. However, I did not do any evil actions with my body. Because of this, my body is beautiful but my mouth is full of worms.

You have seen this with your own eyes, Narada Bhante. The wise and compassionate Buddhas have taught about wholesome things. I say the same to you. Never tell lies or break friendships with divisive speech. Then you will be reborn in heaven and enjoy every happiness you desire.

1.4 Advice to a Daughter

Consoling a crying daughter, the Supreme Buddha gives advice after an alms giving.

Unselfish people give gifts to virtuous people with the intention of sharing merits with departed relatives in the ghost world, or with deities who live in their own houses.

They will receive great benefit, those who share their

merits with the deities Kuvera, Dhatarattha, Virupakkha and Virulhaka—the powerful Four Great Kings who guard this world.

Weeping, sorrow, and lamentation will not benefit departed relatives in any way. They will remain in the ghost world no matter how much we cry.

The merits shared from the donations given to the noble disciples of the Buddha will be received by the departed relatives right away. They will enjoy happiness for a long time.

1.5 Outside the Walls

The Supreme Buddha gave this sermon to King Bimbisara after an alms offering to the Sangha.

After they have been born in the ghost world, departed relatives will come back to their own houses and stand by the doors. They also stand outside walls and at intersections.

Some people in the family will enjoy delicious food without remembering their departed relatives. Departed relatives are forgotten because of their own bad karma.

Some compassionate people offer delicious food and drink to virtuous people and share merits with their departed relatives saying, "Let this be for our relatives! May our relatives be happy!" Departed relatives gather to these places and highly appreciate the offering. They bless their relatives saying, "May our relatives who compassionately offered us these gifts have long, happy, and healthy lives." The givers also gain good results.

Beings in the ghost world do not farm, herd cattle, trade, buy, sell, or use gold and money. They survive on merits shared by humans. As water that rains on a mountain-top flows down to the bottom, so will the merits shared from the human world reach the beings in the ghost world. Just as streams of water fill the ocean, so will the merits shared from the human world reach the beings in the ghost world. One should share merits with departed relatives recalling, "He gave to me, he worked for me, he was a relative, friend, and companion."

Weeping, sorrow, and lamentation will not benefit departed relatives in any way. They will remain in the ghost world no matter how much we cry.

Great King, the merits shared from the donations given to the noble disciples of the Buddha will be received by the departed relatives right away. They will enjoy happiness for a long time. Sharing merits with departed relatives is a very good habit to develop. You have respected departed relatives and supported the monks. By doing this you have collected much merit which will result in extraordinary happiness for a long time, great King.

1.6 Eater of Five Sons

Upon seeing a ghost, a monk asks,

Monk:

You are naked and very ugly. Your body is very smelly. You are surrounded by flies. You, standing there, who are you?

Ghost:

I am a ghost, sir. I am suffering in the world of Yama. I have done an evil deed as a human and have been reborn in the world of ghosts. Every morning, I give birth to five sons and in the evening another five are born. I eat them all that night. But I will still be hungry. My heart is burning with hunger so much that it is smoking. I get no water to drink. See the disaster that has happened to me.

Monk:

Now what evil deed have you done by body, speech, or mind? What have you done so that you have to eat your own sons?

Ghost:

My husband's other wife was about to give birth. I was extremely jealous of her. With that evil mind, I gave her some medicine that would kill the unborn baby. The two month old embryo flowed out just like blood. The baby's grandmother became very angry with me and called her relatives. She frightened me and made me swear an oath. I told a terrible lie by saying, "If I was the one who killed the baby, I will eat my own sons!"

As a result of that evil deed and the lie I told, I have to eat my sons and be covered by their blood.

1.7 Eater of Seven Sons

Upon seeing a ghost, a monk asks,

Monk:

You are naked and very ugly. Your body is very smelly. You are surrounded by flies. You, standing there, who are you?

Ghost:

I am a ghost, sir. I am suffering in the world of Yama. I have done an evil deed as a human and have been reborn in the world of ghosts. Every morning, I give birth to seven sons and in the evening another seven are born. I eat them all that night. But I will still be hungry. My heart is burning with hunger so much that it is smoking. My mind is never peaceful. I am being tortured and in pain as if burned by fire.

Monk:

Now what evil deed have you done by body, speech, or mind? What have you done so that you have to eat your own sons?

Ghost:

I had two sons who had become teenagers. My sons were strong and I used their strength to disrespect my husband.

My husband became very angry and married another wife. When she became pregnant, I got very jealous of her. With that evil mind, I gave her some medicine that would kill the unborn baby. The three month old embryo flowed out just like blood. The baby's grandmother became very angry with me and called her relatives. She frightened me and made me swear an oath. I told a terrible lie by saying, "If I was the one who killed the baby, I will eat my own sons!"

As a result of that evil deed and the lie I told, I have to eat my sons and be covered by their blood.

1.8 The Ox

A son is crying over the death of his ox. His father questions him:

Father:

Are you crazy son? Why are you trying to feed grass to a dead ox saying, "Eat, eat!"? Food and drink will not make it come back to life. You are childish, a fool, and an idiot.

Son:

But father, there are these legs, this head, this body with its tail, and the eyes are the same—this ox might come back to life. But our dead grandfather's hands, legs, body, and head are not seen. But yet you still cry over the pile of earth that was built over his body. Is it not you that is foolish?

Father:

My heart was burning with sadness over the death of my father like when ghee is poured onto a fire. But now, all my sorrow has been extinguished as if I had been sprayed with water. I was struck with an arrow of grief, but you have removed it from me, my son. Having heard your advice, I have become tranquil and cool, with the arrow of sorrow removed. I no longer grieve or weep.

If someone feels compassion towards others, they should try to help them escape from sorrow like the son Sujata to his father.

1.9 Master Weaver

A monk sees a ghost and discusses his experience with others.

Monk:

She eats excrement, urine, blood, and pus. Why does she do this? What has she done for her to have to always feed on blood and pus? New clothes which are very clean, soft, and beautiful turn to hard metal plates when they are given to her. What bad karma has this woman done?

Man:

She was my wife. She was very greedy, mean, and never gave
to anyone. When I offered gifts to monks, she would insult
me. She cursed me saying, "As you offer food, let this food
return to you in the form of excrement, urine, blood, and
pus! As you offer clothes, let these clothes return to you in
the form of metal plates!" Since she had this evil mind, she
now suffers in the ghost world eating filth for a long time.

1.10 Dressed in Hair

A group of merchants sees a ghost and asks,

Merchant:

Who are you, the one staying in that mansion? Why don't
you come out? My dear, we would like to see you and your
psychic powers.

Ghost:

I am naked and embarrassed to come outside. I wear my hair
as my only clothes. I have collected only a small amount of
merit in my previous life.

Merchant:

Alright my dear, I will give you my cloak. Put it on and come
outside. We would like to see you.

Ghost:

I cannot receive what is given by your hand directly to mine.
But within your group, there is a lay follower of the Supreme
Buddha who is very faithful to him and his teachings. Offer
him the cloak and share the merits with me, then I will be
happy and have all the comforts I desire.

Those merchants washed the lay follower and offered him the cloak. They then shared the merit with the ghost.

The ghost received the result instantaneously in the form of food, clothing, and drink. This is the result of the sharing of merit. Then she became pure, wearing the cleanest and finest clothes. Smiling, she came out from the mansion saying, "This is the fruit of your gift."

Merchant:

Your mansion is very beautiful and shines very brightly. Oh devata, tell us what good karma is this the result of.

Ghost:

When I was living in the human world, a monk was going on his alms round. I had a very confident mind towards him and offered an oil cake. As a result of that good karma, I have lived happily in this mansion for a long time. But that result will come to an end soon. In four months, I will die and fall to the very scary and terrible hell. That hell has four corners and four doors. It is divided into sections, surrounded by an iron wall and covered by an iron roof. Its iron floor is glowing with heat. Flames cover the area for hundreds of miles. I will experience pain there for a very long time as the result of my evil deeds. Because of this I am very sad.

1.11 The Elephant

A monk sees a group of gods and another group of ghosts and asks these questions:

Monk:

The deva leading the gods is riding a white elephant. There is a deva in the middle of the line sitting on a chariot. At the end of the line, a female deva travels on a golden stage which shines brightly in ten directions. But you ghosts are carrying hammers in your hands with sad faces and broken bodies. You also drink each other's blood. What bad karma have you done in the human world?

Ghost:

The one in front, riding a white elephant was our eldest son. Having given alms to monks, he is now happy and delighted.

The one in the middle, sitting on a chariot was our second son. He was unselfish and very generous. He now shines brilliantly.

The female deva with soft eyes like a deer's who is at the end, travelling on a golden stage is our youngest daughter. She was wise and donated half of her wealth. She is now happy and delighted.

In the human world, our children gave alms to monks with very pleasant minds. But we were very selfish and insulted monks. Our children are now very happy because they practiced generosity, but we are suffering like withered bamboo reeds.

Monk:

You are suffering today because you missed the opportunity to do good deeds when you had plenty of food and wealth. Now in the ghost world, what kind of food do you eat and what kind of bed do you sleep on? How do you live here?

Ghost:

We hate each other. When we fight each other using hammers, we drink the blood and pus of our victims. But we are still hungry.

Some rich people neither use their wealth nor do meritorious deeds. These greedy people are reborn in the ghost world and suffer.

These ghosts experience the results of their bad karma, suffering from hunger and thirst; they are burning from suffering.

Wealth and property are temporary things. Even this life is very short. Wise people should understand this impermanent nature of life and should seek a way to protect themselves.

There are wise people who understand the Dhamma well. Having heard the teachings of Arahants, they do not forget to give alms.

1.12 The Snake

A beloved son of a family died but none of the family members cried at his death. The son, reborn as the god Sakka, came to the family disguised as an old man and asked them why they didn't cry.

Father:

Just as the serpent sheds its old skin and abandons it, humans also abandon their useless body and die. That burning dead body is unaware of the lamentation of its relatives. Therefore I do not cry over my dead son. He went to another life according to his karma.

Mother:

He came to this world without invitation and departed without permission. He was born in this world and went from this world according to his own karma. What is the use of crying? That burning dead body is unaware of the lamentation of its relatives. Therefore I do not cry over my dead son. He went to another life according to his karma.

Sister:

If I would cry, I would become very exhausted. What would I gain from crying? My crying would only bring more sadness to our relatives, friends, and family. That burning dead body is unaware of the lamentation of its relatives. Therefore I do not cry over my dead brother. He went to another life according to his karma.

Wife:

Just as a child cries asking for the moon, it is the same as someone crying over another's death. That burning dead body is unaware of the lamentation of its relatives. Therefore I do not cry over my dead husband. He went to another life according to his karma.

Servant:

Just as a shattered pot cannot be fixed, it is the same as someone crying over another's death. That burning dead body is unaware of the lamentation of its relatives. Therefore I do not cry over my dead master. He went to another life according to his karma.

2. The Ubbari Chapter

2.1 Sariputta Bhante Helps a Ghost

Sariputta Bhante sees a female ghost and asks,

Sariputta Bhante:

You are naked and very ugly, your veins are popping out. You thin person, with your ribs sticking out, who are you?

Ghost:

I am a ghost, sir. I am suffering in the world of Yama. I have done an evil deed as a human and have been reborn in the world of ghosts.

Sariputta Bhante:

Now what evil deed have you done by body, speech, or mind for you to have been born in the world of ghosts?

Ghost:

Nobody had sympathy for me. Neither my father, mother, nor relatives encouraged me to give alms to monks. Therefore, I did not give alms. I must wander around the world naked and always hungry for five hundred years. This is the result of my evil deed.

I pay respect to you good sir with a very happy mind. Please have compassion towards me, oh noble monk. Please offer something and share the merits with me. Please release me from this state of misery.

Sariputta Bhante:

Very well.

Out of kindness Sariputta Bhante offered a handful of rice, a piece of cloth and a bowl of water to monks. He then shared the merits with the female ghost. The result of that merit was received by the female ghost immediately in the form of food, drink, and clothing. She became clean and fresh with the cleanest and finest clothes. She approached Sariputta Bhante.

Sariputta Bhante:

Who are you, with heavenly beauty, shining in all directions like a star? Why are you so beautiful? What merit have you collected when you were a human?

Ghost:

Sariputta Bhante, you were very compassionate when you saw me in a miserable state: thin, starved, and naked with rough skin. You offered the monks a handful of rice, a piece of cloth, and a bowl of water then dedicated the merit to me.

Now look at the result of offering a handful of rice. For a thousand years I will eat delicious food whenever I want.

Look at the result of offering a piece of cloth. I have as many clothes as King Nanda. Still I have more clothes than that, made from silk, wool, linen, and cotton. There are lots of expensive clothes, so many they even hang from the sky. I can wear whatever I want.

Look at the result of offering a bowl of water. I have gained a beautiful pond with clear and cool water. It is surrounded by fine sand and there are fragrant lotuses and lilies with flower petals floating in the water. I am very happy playing in the water. I am not afraid of anything. You were very compassionate to me Bhante. I have come to worship you.

2.2 Sariputta Bhante's Mother

Sariputta Bhante sees a female ghost and asks,

Sariputta Bhante:

You are naked and very ugly. Your veins are popping out. You thin person, with your ribs sticking out, who are you?

Ghost:

I was your mother in a previous life. Now I am living in the ghost world suffering from hunger and thirst. My food is saliva, mucus, phlegm, the fat of burning bodies, the blood of women giving birth, blood of wounds, pus, and the blood from shaving wounds. I can only feed on the pus and blood of humans and animals. I do not have of a house of my own, therefore I stay in the cemetery. Oh my son, please offer alms to monks and dedicate that merit to me. Then I will be free from eating pus and blood.

Having heard what his mother said, the compassionate Sariputta Bhante called Moggallana Bhante, Narada Bhante, and Kappina Bhante. Sariputta Bhante built four huts and offered those huts along with food and drink to the whole community of monks and dedicated the merit to his mother.

The result of this donation immediately took effect in the form of food, drink, and clothing for the ghost. She became pure, wearing the cleanest and finest clothes with jewelry. Then she approached Moggallana Bhante.

Moggallana Bhante:

Who are you, with heavenly beauty, shining in all directions like a star? Why are you so beautiful? What merit have you collected when you were a human?

Ghost:

I was your mother in a previous live. I was reborn in the ghost world suffering from hunger and thirst. My food was saliva, mucus, phlegm, the fat of burning bodies, the blood of women giving birth, the blood of wounds, pus, and the blood from shaving wounds. I could only feed on the pus and blood of humans and animals. I did not have a house of my own, therefore I stayed in the cemetery.

I am very happy now, rejoicing in Sariputta Bhante's gift. I do not fear anything. I have come here to worship the compassionate Sariputta Bhante.

2.3 The Ghost Matta

A housewife named Tissa sees a female ghost and questions,

Tissa:

You are naked and very ugly, your veins are popping out. You thin person, with your ribs sticking out, who are you?

Matta (ghost):

My name is Matta, and you are Tissa. Don't you remember? I was your husband's other wife. I did lots of evil actions and was born in the ghost world.

Tissa:

Now what evil deed have you done by body, speech, or mind for you to have been born in the world of ghosts?

Matta:

I got angry easily and spoke harshly. I was very jealous, greedy, and cunning. Having used harsh words, I have been reborn in the world of ghosts.

Tissa:

Oh yes, I remember you. You were very violent those days. Let me ask you something else. Why are you covered in dirt?

Matta:

Do you remember one day, you had bathed and dressed in clean clothes? I wanted to be more beautiful than you, so I wore a more beautiful dress than yours. But I saw our husband talking and paying more attention to you rather than me. I was extremely jealous and got angry. I took some dirt from the ground and threw it at you. As a result of that bad deed, now I am covered in dirt.

Tissa:

Oh yes, I remember that day you threw dirt at me. Now let me ask something else. Why are you scratching your entire body?

Matta:

One day we both went into the forest to gather some medicinal herbs. You brought back medicinal herbs but I brought back plants that would make the body itchy. Secretly, I scattered them over your bed. As a result of that bad action, my body is always itchy.

Tissa:

Oh yes, I remember that morning when my body got very itchy. Here's another question. Why are you naked?

Matta:

One day, when friends and relatives gathered for a party, you and our husband were invited while I was not. I was very jealous and stole the clothes that you were going to wear to the party. This is why now I am naked.

Tissa:

Yes, yes, I remember when you stole my clothes that night. I have another question. Why do you smell of excrement?

Matta:

You had nice perfumes, cosmetics, and necklaces made of flowers. I threw them into a pile of excrement. This is why now I am very smelly.

Tissa:

Yes, I also remember when I found my perfumes, cosmetics and flower necklaces in a pile of excrement. I would also like to ask you, why do you suffer so much?

Matta:

The wealth in our house was equally shared among us. But I did not collect much merit, therefore I have to suffer now. You warned me saying, "You are doing evil things. Happiness will not come from evil!"

Tissa:

You mistook me for an enemy when I was trying to help. You were also very jealous of me. Now you can see the result of your evil. You had maids and servants in the house and plenty of jewelry, but now they are used by others. Wealth is not eternal.

Bhuta's father is coming home from the market soon, maybe he will give you something. Do not go anywhere; wait until he comes.

Matta:

I am naked and very ugly with veins popping out. It is embarrassing for a woman to be like this. Do not let Bhuta's father see me.

Tissa:

Ok then, what can I give or do for you which can make you happy and gain what you want.

Matta:

Invite four monks as a group and four individually. Offer alms to these eight monks and dedicate the merit to me. Then I will be happy and gain what I want.

Tissa:

Ok, I will.

She offered alms and robes to eight monks and dedicated the merit to Matta. The result of this donation immediately took effect in the form of food, drink, and clothing for the ghost. She became pure, wearing the cleanest and finest clothes with jewelry and then approached Tissa.

Tissa:

Who are you, with heavenly beauty, shining in all directions like a star? Why are you so beautiful? What merit have you collected when you were a human?

Matta:

My name is Matta, and you are Tissa. Don't you remember? I was your husband's other wife. I did lots of evil actions and was born in the ghost world. But I am very happy now, rejoicing in your gift. I do not fear anything.

May you live long, my sister, happily with all your relatives!

Tissa:

Yes sister, one should practice the Dhamma and be generous by giving alms. The person who does this will be reborn in heaven where there is no sorrow.

2.4 The Ghost Nanda

Nandasena sees a ghost and questions,

Nandasena:

You are very dark and ugly with red eyes and black teeth.
You look very nasty. I don't think that you are a human.

Nanda (ghost):

Oh Nandasena, I am Nanda. I was your wife in the human
world. Since I did lots of evil things, I was reborn in the
ghost world.

Nandasena:

What bad things did you do by body, speech, or mind in
order to be reborn in the ghost world?

Nanda:

When I lived with you in the human world, I was very cruel
to you by speaking harshly. I did not respect you at all. That
is why I was reborn in the ghost world.

Nandasena:

Here, I will give you my cloak to wear and then we can go
back home. You can have beautiful clothes, food, and drink
there. Also, you can see your sons and daughters-in-law.

Nanda:

Sadly, I cannot receive anything that is given directly by
your hands. But you can help me by giving alms to virtuous
monks who know the Dhamma well and are free from
passion. Share the merit that you gain with me, and then I
will be happy with all the comforts in the world.

*Nandasena agreed and offered food, drink, shelter, robes,
umbrellas, flowers, and incense to virtuous monks and shared*

the merit he collected with the ghost Nanda. The result of this donation immediately took effect in the form of food, drink, and clothing for the ghost. She became pure, wearing the cleanest and finest clothes with jewelry and then approached Nandasena.

Nandasena:

Who are you, with heavenly beauty, shining in all directions like a star? Why are you so beautiful? What merit have you collected when you were a human?

Nanda:

Oh Nandasena, I am Nanda. I was your wife in the human world. Since I did lots of evil things, I was reborn in the ghost world. But now through the gift given by you, I am very happy and do not fear anything.

I bless you. May you live long and happily with your relatives.

Nandasena:

Yes my dear, one should practice the Dhamma and be generous by giving alms. The person who does this will be reborn in heaven where there is no sorrow.

2.5 Mattakundali

A Brahmin was crying over his dead son's grave when he saw a grieving deva who was disguised as a young man.

Brahmin:

My dear child, you are very handsome, wearing polished earrings, garlands, and sandalwood cream. You are weeping, holding your head in your hands in the middle of this forest. Why are you crying so sadly?

Deva:

I have received a bright golden chariot, but it does not have wheels. That is why I am so sad. I am about to commit suicide.

Brahmin:

Oh dear boy, tell me, what kind of wheels do you need? Should they be made of gold, jewels, rubies, or silver? I will give you a pair of wheels made from anything.

Deva:

We can see the sun and moon right here. It would be great if my chariot could have them as wheels.

Brahmin:

Oh, dear boy, you are indeed foolish. You seek something that cannot be obtained. I am sure that you will die from sadness because it is impossible to get the sun and moon as your wheels.

Deva:

But wait a minute. We can see the sun and moon moving in the sky. We can see their color and tracks. But when someone dies, one can never see him again. So, who is more foolish, you or me? You are crying over your dead son, who cannot even be seen, and I am crying over something that can at least be seen.

Brahmin:

Oh, dear boy, what you just said is very true. Of the two of us I am the greater fool. I am crying to get my dead son back, like a childish boy crying to obtain the moon.

My heart was burning with sadness over the death of my son, like when ghee is poured onto a fire. But now, all my sorrow has been extinguished as if I had been sprayed with water. I was struck with an arrow of grief, but you have removed it from me, my dear boy. Having heard your advice, I have become tranquil and cool, with the arrow of sorrow removed. I no longer grieve or weep.

Are you a god, a divine musician, the god Sakka, or someone's son? Who are you?

Deva:

Your son has been cremated in this cemetery. You are weeping over his remains. I am that son of yours. Having done a meritorious deed, I was reborn in the Tavatimsa Heaven as a deva.

Brahmin:

We have never known you to give a small or large gift in charity. We have never known you to observe the Five or Eight Precepts. What kind of meritorious action did you do to go to heaven?

Deva:

Do you remember when I was very sick and lying sadly on a bed outside our house? One day, all of a sudden, I saw the Supreme Buddha who had great wisdom and a pure mind, and who had realized everything about this world.

I was very happy and had confidence when I saw him. I quickly worshiped him. That was the only meritorious action I did to have come to this heaven.

Brahmin:

It is wonderful! Just mere worshiping has resulted in a great happiness. Without delay, on this very day, I happily place confidence in the Buddha. I go for refuge to the Buddha.

Deva:

That is exactly what you should do. From this very day, go for refuge to the Supreme Buddha, the Supreme Dhamma, and the Supreme Sangha with a confident mind. Follow the Five Precepts honestly without breaking any of them.

Stop killing any beings, never steal, never drink alcohol, never lie, never commit sexual misconduct, and be content with your own wife.

Brahmin:

Oh Deva, you really wish for my well-being. You have been very helpful to me. From today onward, you are my teacher. I will do all the things you advised me to do. With a confident mind I go for refuge to the Supreme Buddha, the excellent Dhamma, and the disciples of the Great Teacher – the Noble Sangha. I will stop killing living beings, never steal anything, never drink alcohol, never lie, and never commit sexual misconduct. I will be content with my own wife.

2.6 King Kanha

Minister Rohineyya is helping King Kanha remove sadness over his son's death.

Rohineyya:

Please wake up King Kanha. Why are you lying down? What good do you gain from sleeping? Your brother Ghata, who is as close to you as your heart and right eye, is suffering from a disease. He is crying as if he is crazy, asking for a rabbit.

Having heard this, King Kanha became worried about his brother and got up quickly. He visited his brother and questioned,

King Kanha:

Why are you crying like a crazy man saying, "Rabbit! Rabbit!"? What kind of rabbit do you want? One made of gold, jewels, copper, silver, or precious stones? It doesn't matter, I will make it for you. There are also rabbits in the forest that feed on grass. I will catch them for you. What kind of rabbit do you want?

Ghata:

I don't want any of those rabbits that are on the earth. I need the rabbit that is on the moon. Bring that one down for me, my dear Kanha.

King Kanha:

Dear brother, you are asking for something ridiculous. You will waste your sweet life desiring that.

Ghata:

Oh! My dear Kanha, if you are wise enough to teach me, why are you still crying over your dead son?

Wanting one's son to not die is a wish that cannot be obtained by humans or non-humans in the world. It is impossible to bring the dead back to life by praying or any kind of medicine.

There are people who are very powerful, rich, and rule over kingdoms. Even they are not free from old age and death.

Kings, Brahmins, servants, or low cast people are not free from old age and death. Even ascetics who recite mantras living in forests are not free from old age and death. There are also virtuous and calm rishis; even they leave their body when their time ends.

There are Arahants, who have reached Nibbana, and are free from defilements. They also leave their bodies at the end of the lifespan for the last time.

King Kanha:

My heart was burning with sadness over the death of my son like when ghee is poured onto a fire. But now, all my sorrow has been extinguished as if I had been sprayed with water. I was struck with an arrow of grief, but you have removed it from me, my brother. Having heard your advice, I have become tranquil and cool with the arrow of sorrow removed. I no longer grieve or weep.

The wise people in the world advise others with compassion, just as Ghata helped his elder brother. It was Ghata's advice that freed his elder brother from sorrow. If someone has ministers like King Kanha had, they will gain happiness.

2.7 Wealthy Dhanapala

A group of merchants sees a ghost and questions him.

Merchant:

You are naked and very ugly, your veins are popping out. You thin person, with your ribs sticking out, who are you?

Dhanapala (Ghost):

I am a ghost, sir. I am suffering in the world of Yama. I have done an evil deed as a human and have been reborn in the world of ghosts.

Merchant:

Now what evil deed have you done by body, speech, or mind for you to have been born in the world of ghosts?

Dhanapala:

I was a wealthy merchant named Dhanapala who lived in the city of Erakaccha, one of the Dasannas people. I possessed eighty cartloads of gold, and many others of pearls and precious stones.

Even though I was very rich, I did not give anything to anybody at all. I used to close the doors of my house when I was eating fearing that beggars would come to me. I was rude, greedy, and insulted others. I did not believe in the Supreme Buddha.

I often tried to get in the way of people when they were giving alms by saying, "There is no result from giving. Nothing good comes from following precepts." I destroyed lotus ponds, water pots, gardens, and bridges that were meant for the public.

The only deeds I did were evil ones. After my death, I was reborn in the world of ghosts, suffering from hunger and thirst. It has been forty five years since I left the human world. I do not remember ever having eaten food or having drunk water. This is the result of being greedy.

In the past, I was very foolish. I did not give anything even though I was rich, even though there were many opportunities to give. I did not collect merits for the protection of my future lives. Now I regret my previous evil actions.

Four months from now, I will die and fall to the very scary and terrible hell. That hell has four corners and four doors. It is divided into sections, surrounded by an iron wall and covered by an iron roof. Its iron floor is glowing with heat. Flames cover the area for hundreds of miles. I will experience

pain there for a very long time as the result of my evil deeds.
Because of this I am very sad.

Therefore, I warn all of you, do not commit evil deeds either
openly or in secret, because you cannot escape their results,
even if you fly up and run away.

Be respectful to your mother, father, elders in the family, as
well as monks and ascetics. In this way, you will be reborn
in heaven.

2.8 The Ghost Chullasetti

King Ajatasattu sees a ghost and questions him,

King:
You there who is naked and thin, where are you going in the
middle of the night and why? Tell me and I will be able to
give you some food and clothes.

Chullasetti (ghost):
I was a very rich and famous man living in Benares, but I
was evil. I wanted to enjoy my wealth alone so I did not give
anything to others. Through this evil, I was reborn in the
world of ghosts.

I am very hungry. I feel like I am being pierced by needles. I
go to my relatives to receive the merits they share and get
some food. But unfortunately they do not give alms and do
not believe that there is any good result from giving to be
experienced in the next world.

Luckily my daughter always says, "I will give alms and
dedicate the merit to my father and grandfathers." Now she

is going to offer alms to Brahmins and I am going to the city of Andhakavinda to receive the merit and eat something.

King:

After you have gone there to eat, come back here because I also want to help you. I believe what you say.

The ghost departed. Only Brahmins came to that alms giving. There were no noble disciples of the Supreme Buddha. Therefore the result of the merit was not powerful. The ghost came back to the city of Rajagaha and appeared in front of the king.

King:

Tell me what you need, I will give you anything that will make you happy for a long time.

Ghost:

Please offer food, drink, and robes to the Supreme Buddha and the monks who follow him, then dedicate the merit to me. That way I will live happily for a long time.

The king left the palace to meet the Buddha and offered alms. He told the story of the ghost to the Buddha and shared the merits with the ghost.

Having received the merit, the ghost became bright and very beautiful. He appeared in front of the king.

Ghost:

I am now very happy and possess many luxuries. Even humans do not have this kind of happiness. Look at the power of that merit you shared with me by giving alms to the Buddha and his disciples. Great King, you have been very helpful to me. Now I can always live happily.

2.9 The Merchant Ankura

A group of merchants tries to capture a ghost.

Ankura (merchant):
We are going to the country of Kamboja to do business. This god will help us get what we want. Let's take him with us.

After we have taken the god, either with his permission or by force, we will put him on a cart and can go quickly to the city of Dvaraka.

Ghost:
One should not break the branches of a tree which he previously rested under. It is like injuring a friend, this is a very evil deed.

Ankura:
Dear god, it doesn't matter. One should even cut down the trunk of a tree he previously used for shade if he needs it.

Ghost:
One should not remove even one leaf of the tree that he previously used for shade. It is like injuring a friend. This is a very evil deed.

Ankura:
No, oh god, one should even pull the whole tree out along with the roots if he needs it.

Ghost:
A man should not even have an evil thought against another man who helped him by providing food, drink, and shelter, even for one night. Showing gratefulness is always praised by the wise in this world.

A man should not even have an evil thought against another man who helped him by providing food, drink, and shelter, even for one night. Good people with honest hearts do not like to associate with bad friends.

A person who harms another who had previously helped him will not have good fortune.

If one hates another who does not hate him back, the bad karma will come back to that same fool just like when dust is thrown up and falls back down.

I am not easily defeated by a god or man. I have very mighty psychic powers with great beauty and strength. I can travel great distances.

Ankura:
Your hands are golden, five streams of sweet juices flows out of your hand. You must be Sakka, the King of Gods.

Ghost:
No, I am not the god Sakka nor a famous god or gandhabba. I lived in the human world in the city Bheruva. After death, I was reborn in the ghost world. Ankura, I am a ghost.

Ankura:
What good deed did you do when you were living in Bheruva city to get those wonderful hands of yours?

Ghost:
I was a tailor in Bheruva city. Back then, my life was very hard and I had nothing to give. However, my workshop was close to a man named Asayha who was very generous. He was a disciple of the Buddha, followed precepts, and collected lots of merit. Beggars would come to me asking where the house

of wealthy Asayha was, saying, "Blessings to you! Where should we go? Where are the alms given out?" I would point with my right hand and answer saying, "Blessings to you! You should follow that direction. The alms are given out there at Asayha's residence." For this reason, my hand flows with sweet juices.

Ankura:

You did not give alms to anyone with your own hand, but you helped others by pointing to the place where someone else gave alms. For that meritorious deed your hand flows with sweet juices.

I am curious about the generous man who gave those alms. Where was he reborn after death?

Ghost:

I do not know for sure but wherever he is, he must be very powerful and bright. I have also heard from the god Vessavana that he has been reborn in the same heavenly world where Sakka the leader of gods is.

Ankura:

It is really great to do good deeds such as giving alms. After seeing the hand which gives unlimited happiness, why would anyone not collect merits?

Definitely, when I return to the city of Dvaraka, I will give alms which will result in happiness.

I will give food, drink, clothing, and provide houses to stay in. I will build public water tanks, wells, and bridges in places where it is hard to cross.

While this discussion was taking place, suddenly the merchant Ankura saw another ghost and questioned him.

Ankura:

Why are your fingers crooked, your face disfigured and ugly? Why are tears oozing from your eyes? What bad karma did you do for this to happen?

Ghost:

Now, you know about that generous man Asayha, the disciple of the Buddha. He appointed me as the person in charge of gifts in his house. But when I saw beggars who had come asking for food, I did not like to see them, so I would purposely turn my face away from them with anger. For that reason, my fingers and face are now deformed, and tears are oozing out from my eyes. This was the evil deed that I committed.

Ankura:

Oh unfortunate man, you are suffering with crooked fingers and a deformed face because you were unhappy about others giving alms.

I have to be very careful when I appoint somebody else to give alms.

When I leave here and go back to Dvaraka city, I will give food, drink, clothing and houses for travelers. I will build water tanks and bridges in places where it is hard to cross. This will bring me happiness in my future life.

When Ankura returned to Dvaraka, he gave food, drink, clothing and guest houses. He built water tanks, wells, and bridges in places where it was hard to cross. He did all these things with a very happy mind. Every morning and evening, servants and cooks in Ankura's house invited people to his house, calling loudly, "Who is hungry? Who is thirsty? Who needs clothes? Who needs a resting place for their oxen? Who needs an umbrella? Who needs perfumes? Who needs flowers? Who needs sandals?"

Ankura appointed a young man named Sindaka to organize alms. One day, Ankura spoke to Sindaka thus:

Ankura:

My dear Sindaka, the people think that I have a very happy and satisfied life, but if there are little or no beggars that come to my house on some days, I am very sad and will not sleep well.

Sindaka:

If the god Sakka, leader of the Tavatimsa Heaven, was to grant you one wish, what would you wish for?

Ankura:

I would wish:

May heavenly food appear in front of me when I wake up.

May I see virtuous beggars.

May I never be short of things to give.

May I feel no regret after giving.

May I have a very pleasant mind while giving.

At that time, a man named Sonaka was sitting there listening to the conversation, and spoke to Ankura saying,

Sonaka:

One should not give everything one has to others. One should not only give alms, but one should also protect one's own wealth. Therefore wealth is better than giving. Those people who give too much will become poor. Wise people do not praise not giving or giving too much. Giving in a balanced way is always safe.

Ankura:

No Sonaka, I will definitely continue to give to others. May lots of good people become my friends. I want to make everyone happy. I want to give gifts to them like a cloud that rains everywhere.

When people welcome beggars to their house happily and becomes happy after giving, those people living there will definitely become happy. One should have a pleasant mind before giving, while giving, and after giving. This is the way to collect powerful merit.

Ankura is always thinking about giving. Sixty thousand carts of food are given constantly to the people who come to his house. There are three thousand cooks wearing beautiful jewelry working for Ankura to prepare alms. There are another sixty thousand young men who chop firewood to be used for the cooking fire. There are twelve thousand women wearing beautiful jewelry preparing ingredients for the food. There are another twelve thousand women wearing beautiful jewelry standing with spoons to distribute the food.

In this way, King Ankura gave an immeasurable gift of alms to many people. He gave alms again and again in a very organized way, with respect and with his own hands. He gave alms for many days, months, seasons, years—for a very long time.

Having given such great alms for a long time, after death, Ankura was reborn in the Tavatimsa Heaven.

There was another young man named Indaka who only gave one spoonful of food to the Arahant Anuruddha Bhante.

After death, Indaka was also reborn in Tavatimsa heaven. Surprisingly, Indaka experienced divine happiness with more beautiful forms, sounds, smells, tastes, and tangibles than Ankura. Indaka had a longer life span, beauty, happiness, and power.

One day the Supreme Buddha, the best of men, visited the Tavatimsa heaven and was sitting on the Pandukambala Rock at the foot of the Coral Tree on the top of Mount Meru. A large number of gods assembled there to pay homage to the supreme Buddha. The light of the Buddha's body shone more brightly that those gods.

At that time, Ankura was sitting twelve miles away from the Buddha while Indaka was sitting very close, shining brightly.

The Supreme Buddha noticed both of them and questioned,

Supreme Buddha:
Ankura, why are you sitting far away from me? You have given great alms for a long period of time. Why don't you come closer to me?

Ankura:
There were no noble disciples of the Blessed One to accept my alms so the result was not so fruitful. But Indaka gave very little alms to an Arahant disciple and now shines more brightly than me, like the moon in the midst of stars.

Just like when many seeds are planted in an infertile field, it does not give a large harvest. The farmer will not become happy. In the same way, even though a large alms-giving is given to an ordinary group of people who do not follow the Dhamma and protect precepts, it does not give a big result. It will not make the donor happy.

On the other hand, when a small amount of seeds are planted in a fertile field, it gives a very large and successful harvest. The farmer will be happy. In the same way, if someone offers very little alms to the noble disciples who are virtuous and full of good qualities, the result will be very fruitful.

In order to gain fruitful results from giving, people should give wisely. Then they will be born in heaven.

The Supreme Buddha always praised giving alms wisely. The gifts given to noble disciples give a more fruitful result, just as the seeds planted in a fertile field give a big harvest.

2.10 Uttara's Mother

A female ghost who was very ugly and scary approached a monk who was resting on the bank of the Ganges River. Her hair was extremely long and touched the ground. Covered by her hair, she spoke to the monk.

Ghost:

Bhante, it has been 55 years since I died in the human world. I have not eaten anything or drunk water since then. Please give me some water, I am very thirsty.

Monk:

There is this cool water in the Ganges River flowing down from the Himalayan Mountains. You can take some from here and drink. Why do you ask me for water?

Ghost:

Oh Bhante, if I take water from the river, it turns into blood. That is why I am asking you for water.

Monk:

Now what evil deed did you do by body, speech, or mind so that the water of rivers now becomes blood for you?

Ghost:

I had a son named Uttara who was a disciple of the Supreme Buddha. He donated robes, alms food, shelters, and other supplies to monks. I did not approve of what he did, so I got angry and cursed him by saying, "Hey Uttara, may the food and everything you give be received as blood in your next life!" Because of this action, the water of rivers becomes blood when I take it.

2.11 The Thread Offering

A ghost, in disguise as a human, causes his former fiancé to give string to a monk. He then takes her from the human world to his peta mansion to live for seven hundred years.

Young Woman:

One day a monk came to me needing some string. As a result of offering string to him, I now have beautiful clothes. There are beautiful flowers around this mansion. There are many devas and deities who watch over me. I wear beautiful and divine clothes. I am very comfortable living here; my comforts do not end.

I have received all these pleasures because of that offering of string. Please, noble man, take me back to the human world so I can collect more merits.

Ghost:

It has been seven hundred years since you left the human world. If you go there now, you will appear in the form of a very old woman. All your relatives will have already passed away. What will you gain by going there?

Young Woman:

I have enjoyed these heavenly pleasures for seven hundred years. Please take me to the human world. I want to collect more merit.

The ghost took her by the arm and led her back to the village where she was living and said to her:

Ghost:

You should tell other people that if they want happiness, they need to do meritorious deeds.

Young Woman:

I have seen with my own eyes what happens to those who do not do meritorious deeds. They are sad when they are in the human world and also when they are in the ghost world. But those who do meritorious deeds are happy when they are in the human world and in the heavenly world as well.

2.12 The Dog with the Torn Ears

A king sees a female ghost and says,

King:

In your wonderful garden there are golden stairs. Golden colored sand is spread all over the garden. There are lovely, sweet smelling white water lilies in the pond. There are various kinds of trees in the garden. The garden is covered by the sweet smell of flowers. Swans, herons, geese, and various other birds sing throughout the garden. The trees are full of sweet fruits.

A garden as beautiful as this could not be found anywhere in the human world. These beautiful mansions are made of gold and silver which shines in all directions. There are five hundred divine servants for you. They wear golden bracelets and bangles. There are many beds made of silver and gold covered with comfortable mattresses. You enjoy happiness resting on them.

But surprisingly, you wake up in the middle of the night and go to the garden pond. You are sitting on the bank. Oh, sadly, a dog with torn ears comes to you and eats your flesh until you become a skeleton. Then you go into the pond and your body returns back to normal.

With your body back to normal, you put on beautiful clothes and come to me. What evil deed did you do by body, speech, or mind that a dog eats your flesh every night?

Ghost:

In the city of Kimbila there was a male lay disciple of the Buddha; I was his wife. I was very evil and unvirtuous. I committed sexual misconduct. Having seen my bad character, my husband said to me, "You cheated on me. It is not good for you." When he said this to me, I lied and swore an oath saying, "Oh no! I have not been disloyal to you in body or thought. If I have done bad things, may a dog with torn ears eat my flesh." As a result of my bad action and lie, I have been eaten by a dog with torn ears for seven hundred years.

Great king, by comming here you have helped me very much. I am freed from the dog and have no fear or sorrow. Great king, I pay respect to you, putting my hands together, I beg you to come here to enjoy divine sensual pleasures with me.

King:

My dear, I have already enjoyed divine pleasures with you, now please take me back to my city quickly.

2.13 The Queen Ubbari

There was a wealthy king named Brahmadatta in the city inhabited by the Pancala people. The king had lived a long life and soon died. The king had a wife named Ubbari who often went to his grave and wept saying, "Where are you, Brahmadatta?"

One day, a virtuous ascetic who meditated in the forest visited the cemetery and questioned the people who were gathering there.

Ascetic:

Flowers and incense have been offered to this grave. Who is buried underneath? Why is this woman crying?

People:

Great ascetic, this grave belongs to King Brahmadatta. The woman is his wife crying over her dead husband calling, "Where are you my Brahmadatta?"

Ascetic:

Eighty-six thousand people also named Brahmadatta have been cremated on this same spot. Which one are you crying for?

Ubbari:

Great ascetic, my husband is the son of King Chulani, and also the leader and king of the city Pancala. My husband gave me everything I wanted. I am weeping for my husband Brahmadatta.

Ascetic:

All the kings were also named Brahmadatta, and they were also the son of Chulani. All of them ruled over the city of Pancala. It was also you who were all those kings' wife. Why do you only cry for your last husband and forget the previous ones?

Ubbari:

Great ascetic, was I born only as a woman for such a long time in this journey of Samsara?

Ascetic:

No, you have been born as a woman, man, and animal. The beginning of this long journey cannot be seen.

Ubbari:

My heart was burning with sadness over the death of my husband like when ghee is poured onto a fire. But now, all my sorrow has been extinguished as if I had been sprayed with water. I was struck with an arrow of grief, but you, great ascetic, have removed it from me. Having heard your advice, I have become tranquil and cool with the arrow of sorrow removed. I no longer grieve or weep.

She listened very closely to the words of the ascetic. Taking a bowl and robes, she became a nun. She practiced the meditation of loving kindness in order to be born in the brahma world.

She travelled between villages, towns, and cities and finally passed away in the village called Uruvela. Having practiced thoughts of loving kindness and removed all desires to become a woman, she was reborn in the brahma world.

3. The Small Chapter

3.1 Without Rippling

A minister named Koliya saw a ghost while travelling in a ship and questioned,

Koliya:

Hey ghost, you move through the river Ganges without creating any ripples in the water. Even though you are naked you are wearing flowers and garlands on the upper part of your body unlike a ghost. Where do you live, and where are you going?

Ghost:

I am going to the village of Cundatthika, located between the city of Vasabha and the province of Benares.

With the intention to help the ghost, the famous minister Koliya donated some food and clothes to a barber who was on the ship, and shared the merit with the ghost. Immediately after the donation was given, the ghost received fine clothes and jewelry.

The ghost appeared wearing beautiful clothes, flowers, and garlands. Since the ghost was fortunate enough to be able to receive the merit, he benefited from it. Therefore, people should share merits with their departed relatives repeatedly.

Some ghosts cover their bodies with ragged clothing and some are covered by their hair. They travel in all directions in search of food. Some ghosts will travel for a very long distance only to come back without gaining anything. *They are starving and exhausted, so much so that they would collapse on the ground from their suffering. They suffer as though they are being burned by fire because they did not do good deeds when they were in the human world.*

Ghosts:

We were evil housewives and mothers in the human world. We had plenty of wealth that we could have used to do good deeds, but we were foolish and did not protect ourselves from dangers in our future lives. We had lots of food and drink but we hid it and did not give anything to good monks. We were very lazy and did not have any desire to collect merit. We spent all our time eating and only desired the enjoyment of luxuries. Even when we did give a very small amount of food, we would insult the receiver while we gave it.

Now the houses, servants, and jewelry we had are no longer with us. They belong to somebody else now. The only thing we have now is suffering.

Even if we are born in the human world again, we will be born in very poor, low class families, struggling with great hardship.

In the human world people like us will be poor basket makers and chariot makers doing inferior, low-paying jobs.

Those who are unselfish and generous will be reborn in heaven, in Nandana Park, where they will shine in all the directions and enjoy themselves with all the divine pleasures in Vejayanta Palace. After passing away from there, they will be reborn as humans in very rich, high-class families.

They will be born in families who have all the world's comforts and live in multi-story mansions. They will be cooled by fans made of peacock feathers while sitting on a very comfortable couch. As babies they will be treated very well by many nurses. People decorate the babies with flowers and never let them go from their hands.

This type of life is only for those who were generous in their previous lives. These good-doers rejoice in Nandana Park in the Tavatimsa Heaven without any sorrow.

For those who are selfish, there is no happiness now or in the future, while those who are generous will gain happiness now and in their future lives.

Therefore, those who would like to join these gods should collect lots of merit. Truly they are reborn in heaven and will enjoy happiness there for a very long time.

3.2 The Monk from Mount Sanuvasi

There was once an arahant named Potthapada living in the city of Kundi, on Mount Sanuvasi. He possessed many good qualities.

His mother, father, and brother passed away and were reborn in the ghost world because of the bad deeds they committed in the human world. They were very tired, thin, and naked. They experienced pain as if they were being pierced by needles. They were always scared and would not show themselves.

However, one day the brother revealed himself to Potthapada Bhante while standing on his hands and feet like an animal. But Potthapada Bhante just walked past the ghost without saying anything. The ghost spoke to him saying,

Ghost:

I am your brother who was reborn in the ghost world. Your mother and father are also there right now. Having done evil deeds, now we have to suffer there. They are pierced with needles and are very tired, thin, and naked. They are always scared and do not show themselves.

You are very compassionate, Bhante. Please have pity on us. Please offer alms and dedicate that merit to us. That is the only way we will be happy.

Potthapada Bhante and twelve other monks searched for alms and soon gathered at the same place with the purpose of sharing their meals.

Potthapada Bhante:

Give me the food that you have collected. I want to offer it to the community of monks out of compassion for my departed relatives.

The monks gave their food to Potthapada Bhante. The Bhante offered the food to the Sangha and dedicated the merit to his mother, father, and brother by saying, "Let this merit go to my departed relatives. May my relatives be happy."

The merit he dedicated instantly became a well prepared, good quality curry and other food for the monk's departed relatives. The brother then appeared in front of the monk looking healthy, fresh, and happy, saying,

Brother:

Bhante, there is lots of food for us to eat. But we are still naked. Please do something so we can have some clothes.

Potthapada Bhante then collected some scraps of cloth. Once he had collected enough, he made a robe and offered it to the

Sangha by saying, "Let this merit be for my departed relatives. May my relatives be happy."

The fruit of his donation immediately turned to clothing for his relatives. The brother appeared again in front of the monk dressed in fine clothes and said,

Brother:

There are more clothes here than there are in King Nanda's realm, made from silk and wool, linen and cotton. There are so many that they hang down from the sky. We can wear as many clothes as we want. But we are still homeless, please find a way for us to have a home now.

Potthapada Bhante built a hut from leaves and donated it to the Sangha. When he had offered it, he dedicated the merit by saying, "Let this merit be for my departed relatives. May my relatives be happy." Immediately the merit that he shared came into the form of a large multi-story house.

The brother appeared in front of him once again saying,

Brother:

The house that we have right now cannot be found anywhere in the human world, but it is like the houses where devas live. The house shines in all directions. But Bhante, we are still thirsty. Please find a way to get us some water to drink.

Potthapada Bhante filled a water pot and offered it to the Sangha saying, "Let this merit be for my relatives. May my relatives be happy."

The merit he shared immediately became lotus ponds for the family. These ponds had clear water, beautiful banks, and were filled with sweet fragrance. The water was cool and covered with lotuses, water lilies, and lotus petals.

The relatives of the monk bathed, drank, and enjoyed the water. They then appeared once again in front of Potthapada Bhante saying,

Relatives:

Bhante, we have plenty of water now, but our feet are dried and cracked. We have to walk around on gravel and other sharp objects in our bare feet. Please find a way so we can get something so to ride on.

The elder monk found some sandals and offered them to the Sangha saying, "Let this merit be for my departed relatives. May my relatives be happy." The merit immediately went to the relatives in the form of a carriage. The relatives approached the monk in their carriage and said,

Relatives:

You have shown us compassion, Bhante. You helped us to get food to eat, clothing, houses, water to drink, and vehicles to ride in. We are here now to pay homage to the compassionate Potthapada Bhante.

3.3 The Ghost of Rathakara Lake

A woman was born as a ghost due to previous bad actions. But the results of different good actions arose to her in the form of great luxury. However, she was very lonely. So one day she set out a very sweet fruit to lure people to come to her. A young man found the sweet fruit and went to search for the place that the fruit came from. He saw the ghost and asked her,

Young Man:

Your mansion is supported by many pillars. Countless paintings are inside. When you are in the mansion you shine like the full moon. Your body glows like gold, you are very nice to look at. You are sitting on a beautiful couch decorated with precious jewels.

But you are sitting alone, it looks like you do not have a husband.

There is a lotus pond surrounding your mansion, filled with flowers and lotuses. Golden colored sand is spread around the pond, while mud and duckweed is nowhere to be seen. Beautiful swans glide on the water all the time singing beautiful songs. You are in a ship floating around the pond. You have thick beautiful eyelashes and your face is very delightful, always smiling. You are extremely beautiful, happy, and speak very pleasantly.

This place is perfect, I wish that I could enjoy the heavenly pleasures here with you in this divine park, as beautiful as the Nandana Grove.

Ghost:
If you want to come live with me here collect lots of merit, always keep this place in your mind and never forget it. After death, you will be reborn here and live with me.

Young Man:
Okay, I will do as you say.

The young man performed lots of meritorious deeds. He always thought about the mansion, and after death, he was reborn there and lived with the ghost.

3.4 The Hay Ghost

Monk:

One ghost spreads burning hay on his head while another hits himself on the head with an iron rod. And a third ghost eats his own flesh and blood.

You are eating filthy and disgusting excrement. Why is this happening? Of what evil deeds are these the results?

Ghost:

The ghost putting burning hay on his head injured his mother in the human world, while the one hitting himself on the head with an iron rod was a dishonest and cunning trader. The ghost eating his own flesh and blood stole meat and lied about it to the seller.

For my case, in the human world I was a very bossy housewife who ordered others around in the family. Even though I was capable of giving gifts to others, I was greedy and never gave anything. When people came to my house begging for food, I hid the food and lied by swearing an oath, saying, "There is no food in my house, believe me. If there is any that I have hidden, then let it turn to excrement and I will eat it!"

It is the result of both greed and the fact that I lied. Now good rice turns into excrement when I am about to eat it.

All actions have a result; the results of bad deeds will not simply go away without ripening. Therefore because of my bad deeds I must eat and drink this filthy and disgusting excrement full of worms.

3.5 The Abandoned Baby

Villagers:

The great Buddha's knowledge is wonderful. The Blessed One knows perfectly who has lots of merit and who does not.

This baby has been abandoned in the cemetery. He survives by drinking milk oozing out of his thumb. Demons and non-humans will not harm him. This is because the baby has previously done many meritorious deeds.

Dogs lick his feet to clean them, while crows and jackals protect him. Flocks of birds remove the impurities from his birth, and crows wipe of the dirt from his eyes.

There are no parents or relatives to protect him, to provide him with medicine, or to celebrate his birth.

Being in such a horrible state—abandoned, cold and shivering—his survival is uncertain.

The extremely wise Supreme Buddha, teacher of gods and humans, saw him and announced,

Supreme Buddha:

This baby will become a member of a high-cast family with great wealth.

Villagers:

What has the baby done in his previous life to get this result? Having fallen to a miserable state, how would this baby become a member of a high cast family?

Supreme Buddha:

In his previous life, he insulted a group of people who were giving alms to the monks headed by the Buddha, and he spoke harshly to the Buddha and the monks.

Afterwards, he abandoned that evil mind. Becoming a devoted disciple, he developed a happy mind towards the Supreme Buddha and monks. Furthermore, he offered rice-gruel to the Supreme Buddha for seven days.

These were his good actions. That is why even though he is miserable now, he will be very wealthy and happy in the future.

He will live in this world for one hundred years as a very wealthy and happy person and after death be reborn in the Tavatimsa Heaven with the god Sakka.

3.6 The Ghost Serini

Man:
You are naked, ugly, and very thin. Your ribs and veins are sticking out from your body. Who are you?

Female Ghost:
I am a ghost. I did evil deeds when I was in the human world. As a result, I have to suffer in the ghost world.

Man:
What evil deed have you committed by body speech or mind to make you suffer here?

Female Ghost:
In the human world, I had plenty of wealth and many opportunities to collect merit. But I was very greedy and did not give anything to anybody.

Now, as a result of my greed, if I get close to a river to drink, the river appears empty to me and full of sand. As I go towards the shade of a tree to rest, the spot becomes scorched by the sun. The wind feels like fire blowing on me, burning me. But I deserve all these sufferings because I have done lots of evil.

Please, could you go to the city of Hatthinipura, find my mother and tell her, "I have seen your daughter reborn in the miserable world of Yama because she did evil deeds."

And also tell her that I collected four hundred thousand coins and hid them under the couch I slept on. I have not told anyone about it.

Ask her to take the money and use it for giving alms in my name. She should dedicate the merit of this gift to me. Then I will be happy and get whatever I want.

Man:
Very well.

The man went to the city of Hatthinipura, found the mother of the female ghost and spoke to her thus:

Man:
I have seen your daughter reborn in the miserable world of Yama because she did evil deeds. She told me to tell you that she has collected four hundred thousand coins and hid them under the couch she slept on. She has not told anyone about them.

She wants you to use that money for giving alms in her name. You should dedicate the merit of this gift to her. Then she will be happy and get whatever she wants.

The mother used the money to offer alms to monks and assigned the merit of the donation to her. The ghost became very happy and had a very beautiful body.

3.7 The Deer-Hunter

Man:

You are young and surrounded by male and female deities. You look very happy with all the pleasures that you have. But in the daytime, you experience very painful feelings. What did you do in your previous life?

Ghost:

I was a cruel deer hunter living in the city of Rajagaha. I was always looking for something to kill. I did not have any pity on innocent beings.

I had a friend who was very compassionate, a disciple of the Supreme Buddha. He always said, "Do not do evil deeds my friend; do not be reborn in a bad world. If you wish to go to a happy world after death, then stop killing living beings."

I did not listen to his advice because I took pleasure in killing and was very foolish.

My friend again advised me saying "If you must kill in the daytime, then please at least stop killing at night."

So I killed living beings in the daytime and stopped during the night.

That is why I enjoy heavenly pleasures at night, but in the day, dogs come and tear off my flesh.

Even though I only refrained from killing at night, I still gained good results from it. Now I imagine the disciples of the Supreme Buddha who practice the Dhamma diligently throughout their lives surely will attain the supreme bliss of Nibbana.

3.8 A Second Deer Hunter

Man:

In a multi-story mansion you rest on your very comfortable couch, listening to the sweet music of instruments. But at the end of the night before sunrise, you walk towards the cemetery where you experience very painful feelings. What evil deed have you committed by body, speech, or mind that you suffer like this?

Ghost:

In the city of Rajagaha, I was a hunter who was very cruel and had no self-control. I had a very kind friend who was a lay follower of the Supreme Buddha. He felt pity for me and kept advising me again and again, saying, "Do not do bad deeds my friend; do not be reborn in a bad world. If you wish to be reborn in a good world, then stop yourself from killing living beings.

I did not listen to his advice because I took pleasure in killing and was very foolish.

My friend who felt sorry for me advised me again saying, "If you have to kill living beings in the daytime, then please stop yourself from doing so at night."

So I killed living beings during the daytime and stopped during the night. Because of this, I enjoy heavenly pleasures during the night and during the day, dogs come and eat me.

Even though I only restrained myself from killing at night, I still gained good results from it. Now I imagine the disciples of the Supreme Buddha who practice the Dhamma diligently throughout their lives will surely attain the supreme bliss of Nibbana.

3.9 The Back Biter

Narada Bhante:

You are wearing many garlands, a crown, and many other types of jewelry on your hands and legs. Your body is covered with sandalwood cream. Your facial expression is very pleasant and your body shines very brightly just like the sun.

You are surrounded by ten thousand divine maidens who serve you whatever you want.

They wear bracelets and have golden wreaths on their heads. You look very mighty and your appearance is very majestic. When people look at you they are stunned by your appearance and their body hairs stand on end.

But you eat the flesh off your own back. What evil deed have you committed by body speech or mind to make you eat your own flesh?

Ghost:

When I was living in the human world I lied, broke friendships using divisive words, cheated others, and did lots of cunning deeds. In the middle of large gatherings of people, when I was asked to tell the truth, I lied.

I insulted others behind their backs. As a result of speaking behind others backs, today I have to eat the flesh off my own back.

You have seen how I am suffering, Narada Bhante. Now I see the truth of the words of the wise and compassionate Buddhas. I can tell you now, do not break friendships, do not tell lies, and may you not have to eat the flesh off your own back like I do!

3.10 Insulting the Relics Puja

Monk:

While you are floating in the air, a bad smell comes out of you. Worms are eating your mouth. What evil deed did you do in your previous life?

Afterwards, a group of ghosts slice your mouth with knives. They slice again and again placing salt on the wounds. What evil deed did you commit by body, speech, or mind in your previous life? What is that the result of?

Ghost:

In the city of Rajagaha I was an extremely wealthy person. One day my wife, daughter, and daughter-in-law were ready to go to worship a stupa that held relics of the Buddha. They had prepared lotus flowers, garlands made of flowers, and incense. I stopped them from going there. That was the evil deed I did.

There are about eighty-six thousand ghosts here suffering each in their own way. They all committed the same evil deed of insulting the worshipping of the Buddha's relics. We are suffering intensely in this ghost world as if we were in hell.

If one criticizes worshipping the relics of the Supreme Buddha, that person loses a great meritorious opportunity.

Look at those female deities travelling in the sky, decorated with garlands and flowers. They enjoy this great happiness as a result of offering flowers to the relics of the Supreme Buddha. Having seen this marvelous, amazing, and hair raising result of merit, wise people salute and pay homage to the great sage, the Buddha.

When I am released from this ghost world and reborn in the human world, I will diligently worship again and again the stupas of the relics of the Supreme Buddha.

4. The Large Chapter

4.1 King Ambasakkhara

In the city of the Vajjian people named Vesali there was a Licchavi king named Ambasakkhara. One day while he was outside of the city, he went to see a prisoner who was impaled on a sharp stake. There, the king saw a ghost. The king questioned the ghost,

Ambasakkhara:

This person can neither sleep nor sit. He cannot even take a step backwards or forwards. There are no clothes for him to wear or food to eat. He previously had relatives and friends but now there is nobody to help him, as if he has been thrown away. Friends will stay close to you when you are rich but abandon you when you are poor.

Having lost all of his possessions, now he is suffering with broken limbs and bleeding body. His life is uncertain, like a dew drop about to fall. He is about to die either today or tomorrow. Seeing such an unfortunate being, why do you say "May he live, may he live! Living is better than dying"?

Ghost:

Great King, when I recollected my past lives, I understood that he was my relative in a previous life. I had compassion towards him thinking, "Do not let his bad karma drag him into hell."

Great King, if he dies he will fall into a very hot, severe, and frightful hell named Sattussada. This stake that he is on right now is countless times better than that terrible hell. Now if he were to know about what I just said, he would be afraid and lose his life. That is why I do not tell him about this.

Ambasakkhara:

I understand the situation that this person is in. Now I want to know about another thing too. Please give us permission to ask and do not get angry with me.

Ghost:

In the past, I had decided not to tell anyone who does not believe in karma about the ghost world. But now, since you have some trust in me, I will answer reluctantly. Ask anything you wish.

King:

Friend, I can believe whatever I see with my eyes. If I do not believe what I have seen with my eyes, then you can criticize me.

Ghost:

Please keep your promise. Now I will teach you the Dhamma. Listen carefully with an open and happy mind. Maybe you have heard the things I am about to say or maybe not, but I will tell everything I know.

King:

You have come here in a magnificent carriage pulled by white horses. It is very amazing and beautiful. Of what deed is this the result?

Ghost:

When I was in the human world I lived in the city of Vesali. One day there was a muddy area on a road. I placed the skull of an ox on that muddy area so that others could easily pass stepping on it. This was the good deed for which I have received this magnificent carriage.

King:

Friend, your body shines in all directions and the fragrance of your body spreads everywhere. You have divine psychic power too, but you are fully naked. What is the reason for this?

Ghost:

In the human world, my heart was free from anger and filled with kindness. I always talked to people with gentle speech. From this deed I gain my heavenly radiance. When I saw people who were following the Dhamma, I admired them and congratulated them. From this deed sweet fragrance spreads from my body.

One day, however, while my friends were bathing in a river, I playfully took their clothes and hid them without any evil thoughts in my mind. For this reason, I am now naked and I suffer.

The Buddha has taught that such will be the result if one commits a bad deed for fun. He has also taught how serious the consequences will be for those who commit evil deeds with bad intentions.

Those people who commit bad deeds with bad intentions by body, speech, and mind will surely go to hell after death.

But those who are very generous and kind to others will surely go to heaven after death.

King:

Now you have explained about good and bad karma, but how do I believe that there are results of good and bad deeds? Having seen what, should I believe it? Who can convince me about this?

Ghost:

When you have seen or heard the results of karma, you should believe in it. You must believe that this is the result of doing good and evil deeds. Otherwise, if there were no results of good or bad actions, why do some beings go to bad worlds and some to good worlds? What is the reason that some beings are poor and some are rich? Since living beings do good or bad deeds, they have happy or miserable existences and births in low or high classes.

I have now explained the actions that lead to happiness and the actions that lead to suffering. Doers of good rejoice in heaven. The fools who do not believe in the results of good and bad actions suffer in hell.

I have not done any meritorious deeds and there is nobody who will share their merits with me so that I can have clothes, houses, foods and drink. For this reason I am suffering with a naked body.

King:

Is the any way for you to get clothing? Tell me a way so that I can give you clothes. I will believe in your words.

Ghost:

There is an Arahant monk named Kappinaka nearby. He is

very virtuous and restrained in senses. His speech is very pleasant and he is a very skilled preacher. He meditates and is free from all defilements. He has become very calm and has realized the true nature of life. He is very gentle, tranquil, free from desires, concentrated and very wise. He has attained the triple knowledge. He is worthy of offerings from gods and humans.

Not many people know about his achievements. People cannot easily recognize him as an Arahant. People in the Vajjian state call him a sage. Powerful gods and yakkhas praise his qualities everywhere saying, "The Arahant monk Kappinaka is a great sage, free of passion."

Please go and meet that Bhante and offer him a pair or two of robes. If he accepts them, and if you dedicate the merit to me, you will then see me with beautiful clothes.

King:
Where is that monk staying right now? Will he help me get rid of my doubts and wrong views?

Ghost:
He is resting at the village of Kapinaccana surrounded by many gods. He preaches the beautiful and excellent Dhamma which he practices very well.

King:
Yes, certainly I will go there right now and offer two robes and dedicate the merit to you. Then I will see you with beautiful clothes.

Ghost:
Wait, you should find another time to visit him because it is not good to disturb his meditation.

King:

Yes I will find a better time.

Surrounded by servants, the king then left that place and returned to his palace in the city. In the morning he bathed and ate his breakfast. He chose eight pairs of clothes from his closet and had the servants carry them. When the time was right, the king went to the place where the monk was. The monk was very calm and tranquil, seated at the foot of a tree. He had just returned from his morning alms round. The king approached him, asked about his wellbeing, and further said,

King:

Venerable Bhante, I am a Licchavi king from the city of Vesali. People know me as Ambasakkhara of the Licchavi clan. Please sir, accept these eight pairs of clothes of mine. I am offering these to you. I would be delighted if you accept them.

Monk:

Monks try to avoid your home. You break their bowls and even tear up their robes. Your people kick and trip them so they fall on their heads. These are the harassments that are caused by you and your people.

You have given nothing in charity nor have you shown the way to people who are lost. You have even grabbed the stick from a blind person. Being such a greedy and mean person, why are you here offering us robes?

King:

All that you have said about me is true, Bhante. Yes, I have harassed monks, but I have only done these things for fun not with an evil mind. But now I understand, even those deeds are very bad.

I know a ghost who committed an evil deed for fun now experiences suffering. He is a good person, but he is completely naked. What a terrible thing that is.

Bhante, I saw that ghost and I felt very sorry for him. For this reason I am now offering this gift. Please accept these eight pairs of clothes, and may the merit also reach that ghost.

Monk:

Surely, generosity has been praised by the Supreme Buddha. May generous people's wealth increase further. I will accept your clothes and may the ghost share in this merit.

The king washed his face and offered the eight pairs of clothes to the Arahant monk saying,

King:

May Bhante accept these! May I see the ghost wearing beautiful clothes!

The ghost appeared in front of the king. The ghost was surrounded by many servants while sitting on a majestic pure-bred horse. He had a beautiful body covered with the fragrance of sandalwood and wore beautiful clothes.

The king was amazed and delighted when he saw the ghost. He saw with his own eyes the result of his offering.

The king approached the ghost and said,

King:

I will always give gifts to monks. Now there is nothing that I own that I cannot give. You have helped me very much, my friend.

Ghost:

Great king, you have offered one of the four requisites—clothing. It has been very fruitful. Even though I am a non-human and you are human, now we are talking together.

King:

Dear friend, I regard you as my relative, friend, god, and refuge. Worshipping you, I plead: I would like to see you again.

Ghost:

Yes, it can be on one condition. If one day you lose faith in the Dhamma, become very greedy, and follow wrong views, you will not see me anymore. Even if you see me, I will not talk to you.

But if you continuously develop respect for the Dhamma, practices generosity, become very kind and helpful to others, and often donate to monks, you will see me, and when I see you I will talk to you.

Great King, the reason we were able to become friends is because of that man on the stake. So please, release that man as soon as possible.

If the man is quickly released, he may have a chance to live, to do lots of good deeds, and even to escape from hell.

Please go with that man to meet Kappinaka Bhante and offer food and drink. He has to experience the result of another evil deed. Ask the Bhante about this, Bhante will explain everything. You should also listen to Bhante with the intention of understanding the Dhamma and not with a criticizing mind.

The king agreed with the ghost and promised to do as he said.

Then the king went to the council of ministers and asked,

King:

Gentlemen, listen to me please. Do you remember that man who is dying on the stake? It is true that he has done evil deeds. We have already punished him. But he is loyal to the king. It has been twenty nights since he has been tortured on the stake. He is neither dead nor alive. Please give me the permission to release him.

Ministers:

Oh great King, you do not need to ask for permission from us. We will agree with your decision. Soldiers, please release that man.

Quickly, the king went to the prisoner who was on the stake and released him. The king told him not to be afraid. The king instructed his doctors to treat the man. Once the man was cured and healthy, the king took him to see the Arahant monk Kappinaka and they offered food and drink. The king questioned the monk thus,

King:

This man was undergoing punishment on a stake for twenty nights. He was very close to death. He had done evil deeds, but he was a loyal person to the king. Bhante, having listened to the suggestions of a ghost, I have released him. I learned that he would have been born in hell if he had died. Please teach him the way to escape from hell. We will listen to you trusting that you will tell us the truth. Is it possible that the results of some bad karma will disappear without ripening?

Monk:

If he practices the Dhamma diligently both day and night, he will escape from hell. But he will have to suffer the result of that bad karma somewhere else if he does not put an end to the round of rebirth.

King:

Bhante has answered the question that I asked about this man. Now, please have pity on me too. Very wise Bhante, teach me the Dhamma so that I also will escape from hell.

Monk:

You should take refuge in the Buddha, Dhamma, and Sangha at this very moment. Have confidence in the Triple Gem, observe and keep the five precepts honestly.

Abstain from killing living beings right now, stop stealing, do not take intoxicating drinks and drugs, do not tell lies, and be satisfied with your own wife.

In this way, these eight factors (taking refuge in the Triple Gem and observing the five precepts) will give you much happiness.

The disciples of the Supreme Buddha, the monks, are very virtuous, desireless, have pure lives, and know much about the Dhamma. Have a pleasant mind about them. Offer them robes, food, drink, medicine, resting places, beds, and seats. Daily, the merits from these offerings grow.

In this way, you should practice the Dhamma diligently both day and night and you will escape from hell. But you will have to suffer the result of that bad karma somewhere else if you do not put an end to the round of rebirth.

King:

I will take refuge in the Buddha, Dhamma, and Sangha right now, place confidence in the Triple Gem, and observe and keep the five precepts honestly.

I will stop killing living beings right now, will stop stealing, will not take intoxicating drinks and drugs, will not tell lies, and will be satisfied with my own wife.

In this way, I observe these eight factors which lead to true happiness.

I will offer robes, food, drink, medicine, resting places, beds, and seats to the community of monks, the Sangha, who have virtuous and pure lives.

In this way, King Ambasakkhara of the Licchavi clan became a devoted lay disciple of the Supreme Buddha. He started supporting monks carefully with a humble mind.

The prisoner who was on the stake recovered fully and went to Kappinaka Arahant Bhante and became a monk under him. Marvelously, both the king and the prisoner realized the Dhamma.

This is the benefit of associating with noble friends. The friendship of people who know the Dhamma leads to very great results. The prisoner who was on the stake and later became a monk eventually attained Arahantship and King Ambasakkhara became a Stream Entrant.

4.2 The God Serissaka

A meeting took place between the deva Serissaka and some merchants. Please listen to this good story they told.

There was a king named Payasi in the city of Setavya. He was reborn as an earth deva. He lives happily in his mansion. That deva spoke to the merchants.

Deva:

Non-humans live in frightening forests and in deserts where there is little food, drink, and water. Your journey through this desert is very hard. You are about to die in the middle of this sandy place.

In this desert, there are no fruits, roots or any food or drink. There is no way to make a fire. There is only dust and scorching sand. This rough soil is like a scorched iron pot. It is like hell, without any happiness. This place has been haunted by ghosts for a long time. It seems that this land is under a curse of rishis. What are you seeking? Why have you come here? Is it because of greed, or fear, or have you gotten lost?

Merchants:

Dear Deva, we are merchants from the cities of Magadha and Anga. We travel with full carts to the cities of Sindhu and Sovira to earn money.

We could not stand the heat in the daytime. So, looking for a comfortable place for ourselves and out of compassion for our bulls, we rushed here to this place.

We took the wrong road in the night. We are lost and confused like blind men lost in a forest. We do not know where to go. We are stuck in the middle of this desert.

Deva, we have not seen anything like your mansion before. It is excellent. Because we have seen you, we are extremely happy. It is as if we have regained our lives.

Deva:

People travel to lands on the other side of the oceans. They travel through sandy deserts, over bridges made of canes and stakes, and to many more difficult places just to earn money. When you travel to different countries, what kind of things do you see and hear? I would like to learn about those strange things.

Merchants:

Deva, we have never seen or heard about any happiness greater than yours. Your happiness surpasses human happiness in every way. No matter how long we stare, we will never see enough of your mansion. There are pools in the sky with many white lotuses. The surrounding area is filled with trees that do not stop bearing fruit. Divine fragrance can be smelled everywhere. Your mansion is supported by hundreds of pillars made of beryl, crystals, corals, cat's-eye, rubies, and brilliant jewels. There are golden stages decorated with golden railings. This mansion shines in gold and it is well designed with beautiful stairs. It is extremely beautiful.

There is lots of food and drink inside. Many goddesses play musical instruments and sing welcoming songs to entertain you. You enjoy being surrounded by these goddesses. The happiness you experience is beyond words. It is like the wonderful Nalini Palace of King Vessavana. Are you a god, a demon, the god Sakka, or a human? We merchants question you. Tell us who you are.

Deva:

Dear merchants, I am a deva. My name is Serissaka. I am the protector of this sandy desert. I was appointed by King Vessavana.

Merchants:

Deva, have you obtained these wonderful things by chance,

have you created them yourself, or have other gods given them to you? How did you gain all these delightful things?

Deva:

Merchants, I did not obtain these wonderful things by chance, nor did I create them myself. Other devas did not give them to me. I have obtained these things as a result of my own meritorious deeds.

Merchants:

Dear Deva, what kind of religious activities did you perform and what kind of precepts did you follow? What kind of good deed did you do to gain these wonderful things?

Deva:

I was once a ruler in the country Kosala. My name was Payasi. I held the wrong view that there are no results of good and bad actions. I was very greedy and evil. I believed that nothing exists after death.

There was a great monk named Kumara Kassapa who knew the Supreme Buddha's Dhamma well and could preach skillfully. One day, that monk taught me the Dhamma. That was the day he removed my terrible wrong views.

After hearing his sermon, I became a lay follower of the Supreme Buddha. I abstained from killing beings, stealing, drinking alcohol, lying, and was content with my own wife. That was my religious life and those were the precepts I followed. Due to those meritorious deeds, I obtained this wonderful mansion.

Whatever teaching has been preached by the wise is true. Those teachings are not false. Good doers enjoy the results of their actions wherever they go. Evil doers experience grief, lamentation, and misery wherever they go. They will never escape from falling into miserable worlds.

At that moment, the assembly of devas suddenly became very frightened and sad.

Merchants:
Dear Deva, what happened to you and your fellow devas? Why do you suddenly seem sad?

Deva:
Dear merchants, can you see these flowering Mahari trees in this forest spreading divine fragrance and dispelling darkness? After every hundred years, one petal of each flower falls off. That indicates that we devas have been here for one hundred years. I will stay in this mansion only for five hundred years. I know that very well. By then, my life span and merit will be spent. That is why I am very sad.

Merchants:
Dear Deva, having obtained a wonderful, long lasting mansion like yours, what is the point of being sad? If someone has a short lifespan and little merit it makes sense for them to be sad.

Deva:
Dear merchants, you advised me using pleasing words with good hearts. I will protect you. You will be able to go safely to your destination.

Merchants:
We wish to go to the cities of Sindhu and Sovira to earn money. We promise that we will organize a huge ceremony in the name of Serissaka with lots of gifts.

Deva:

Do not organize ceremonies for me. You will get everything you wish for without having to reward me. Stop doing evil deeds and lead a virtuous life.

There is a lay follower of the Buddha in your group. He is very faithful, virtuous, generous, wise, and well-behaved. He is learned in the Dhamma. He is a very happy lay follower with deep wisdom.

He does not tell lies intentionally. He does not even think to kill beings. He does not try to break others' friendships, and he speaks beneficial things wisely. He is very disciplined, obedient, and established in higher virtue. He respects elders and looks after his parents. He has great noble qualities. I think he earns money just to take care of his parents, not to make himself rich. He intends to be a monk after his parents pass away.

He is straight, not crooked, and not deceitful. How could he experience suffering since he is well established in good qualities?

It is because he was in your group that I appeared before you. Therefore, merchants, following the Dhamma is the best protection. If you had come without that lay follower, you could have been destroyed by disasters in this desert like confused blind men. Association with good people is indeed a blessing.

Merchants:

Deva, please tell us, who is that person? What is his name? What is his role among us? We agree that if you appeared here out of compassion for someone, his company is truly a blessing.

Deva:

Yes, he is a servant of yours. He is your barber, Sambhava. He earns money shaving and cutting people's hair. Recognize him as that lay follower. He is a very quiet person. Don't look down upon him.

Merchants:

Dear Deva, we know who you are talking about. We never thought he was such a person. Having heard your praises, we are ready to worship him.

Deva:

Everybody traveling with you – elders, youth, children, and anyone who is greedy, come inside my mansion and see well the results of merits.

Placing the barber in the front, they all rushed behind him saying, "I am next! I am next!" They went inside the mansion as if entering the wonderful palace of the god Sakka.

When it was time to go for refuge, they all cried, "Let me go first!" wanting to become lay disciples of the Supreme Buddha. They abstained from killing, stealing, drinking alcohol, lying, and were content with their own wives. Everyone rejoiced in taking refuge in the Triple Gem. They rejoiced again and again enjoying divine wonders.

Afterwards, they went to Sindhu and Sovira safely and accomplished their goal of making lots of money. They eventually returned to their home city of Pataliputta safely. They went to their own houses, rejoined their wives and children, and organized a great festival called Serissaka. They delighted in this festival together with their families. They also built an assembly hall called Serissaka.

This is the result of association with noble friends, people who practice the Dhamma. Because of a single lay follower a large group of people benefited.

4.3 The Ghost Nandaka

There was a kingdom called Surattha which had a king named Pingalaka. One day, the king went to help King Moriya. Once he was done, King Pingalaka headed back home in the middle of the day. At that time the weather was very hot. Suddenly a path appeared, created by ghosts. The king saw that beautiful path. Unaware of the ghosts who created that path, he addressed the driver,

King:

Driver, that road is beautiful, safe, and peaceful. Please go and follow that road, it will lead us back to Surattha faster.

The king along with his army entered the path and followed it for a while. All of a sudden, one of the soldiers let out a terrifying scream,

Soldier:

Great King, we have taken the wrong path which is scary and hair-raising! We can see the road ahead, but there is no road behind us. I think we have come to an area where ghosts live. The smell of ghosts is thick, and frightful screams can be heard.

The king was afraid and said to the driver in a terrified voice,

King:

Driver, we have taken a wrong path which is scary and hair-raising. We can see the road ahead, but there is no road behind us. I think we have come to an area where ghosts live. The smell of ghosts is thick, and frightful screams can be heard.

Suddenly, the king climbed up on the back of his elephant and looked carefully at the surrounding. He saw a huge banyan tree that provided lots of shade. It looked very beautiful, like a blue cloud.

King:
Driver, look at that! What is that huge thing that looks like a blue cloud?

Driver:
Great King, it is a banyan tree with lots of shade.

The king approached the huge banyan tree and climbed down off his elephant. He and his ministers went to the tree and sat down in the shade. There was a pot filled with water and some sweet oil cakes. Suddenly, a being wearing beautiful jewelry like a god appeared in front of the king and said,

Ghost:
Welcome great King. Your arrival is a blessing. Please drink this water and eat these cakes.

The king with his ministers ate the oil cakes and drank the water. He then questioned the person,

King:
Are you a god, a heavenly musician, or Sakka, leader of the gods? Please tell us who you are.

Ghost:
Great King, I am not a god or a heavenly musician or Sakka, leader of the gods. I am a ghost. I came here from the state of Surattha.

King:

When you were in the human world, what kind of good deeds did you do? How did you gain this divine power?

Ghost:

Listen to me, great King, ministers, and soldiers. I was an evil person from the state of Surattha. I held wrong view, behaved badly, and was very greedy. I insulted others. I stopped people from doing good deeds. I did not let others practice generosity. I held the following wrong views:

- There is no result of giving.

- There is no result of following precepts.

- There are no people called teachers in this world.

- It is impossible for an untamed person to help others.

- All beings are equal.

- There is no point in respecting elders.

- Nothing can be achieved by making effort.

- There is no need to develop energy.

- No one can be purified through good deeds.

- Beings experience happiness and suffering due only to natural law.

- One's mother is not a special person. There is no need to be grateful and respect her.

- One's father is not a special person. There is no need to be grateful and respect him.

- There is no such thing as a brother and sister.

- There is no rebirth after death.

- Supporting and helping others and collecting merits do not give result.

- If someone beheads another, it does not count as killing. It is only putting a sword through the parts of a body.

- The soul of life can never be destroyed. It is like a ball that is five hundred kilometers high. Just like a ball of thread unwinds itself when thrown, it will only keep rolling as long as there is thread. This life is also like that.

- Just like somebody goes from one village to another or from one house to another, this soul goes from one body to another.

- Regardless of whether one is wise or a fool, everyone has to wander in this samsara for eighty-four hundred thousand great eons. Only then would one end this great suffering. It is like the happiness and suffering of beings has been measured from a bucket. There is a limit of how much suffering and happiness a being can receive.

Only realized people understand these things, everyone else is deluded. I held such wrong views in the past. I was so deluded and covered by ignorance. I committed evil deeds, was very greedy, and insulted others.

Six months from now, I will die and fall to the fearful and terrible hell. That hell has four corners, four doors, and is divided into sections. It is encircled by an iron wall with a roof of iron above. It is covered by burning flames for hundreds of miles.

Great King, the complete lifespan of beings in that hell is one trillion (1,000,000,000,000) years. Once they have suffered one hundred thousand years, suddenly they hear a strange sound. This is how they know they have suffered for one hundred thousand years. People who held wrong views, committed evil deeds, and insulted noble ones are boiled in hell for one trillion years. I am destined to suffer in that hell.

That is why I am extremely sorrowful.

Great King—the one who overcomes his enemies and develops his kingdom—may my blessings be with you. Please listen to me great King. My daughter's name is Uttara, she is still in the human world. She protects the five precepts throughout her life and observes eight precepts four times a month. She is not greedy, but instead very generous. She offers alms and leads a very restrained life. She is very humble towards others and always uses pleasant words. Like this she does lots of meritorious deeds.

Most importantly, she is a lay disciple of the Sakyan sage, the glorious Gautama Supreme Buddha.

Just now a virtuous monk, mindful, with his eyes looking down approached the village where she lives. That monk was going from house to house begging for food. Great King, I am very fortunate that my daughter saw that monk. She offered some water and a sweet oil cake to the monk and dedicated the merit to me saying, "Bhante, my father has passed away. May he receive this merit." At that very moment, I received the result of that merit. Now I enjoy wonderful things here, just like Vessavana, the king of gods.

Great and powerful King, listen to me. In this world with its gods, the greatest being is the Supreme Buddha. You, along with your wife and children, should go for refuge to the Supreme Buddha. The Noble Eightfold Path is the only way leading to Nibbana, the end of suffering. You should go for refuge to the Dhamma. The community of monks is very virtuous, well concentrated, and wise. They are the disciples of the Buddha. The Sangha consists of eight individuals and four pairs of persons. Go for refuge to that Sangha.

Abstain from killing beings right now, stop stealing, do not take intoxicating drinks and drugs, do not tell lies, and be satisfied with your own wife.

King:
Yes, I will take refuge in the Buddha, Dhamma, and Sangha right now, and place confidence in the Triple Gem. I will stop killing beings right now, I will stop stealing, I will not take intoxicating drinks and drugs, I will not tell lies, and I will be satisfied with my own wife.

Just as hay is carried away by strong wind and grass is carried away by the current of a stream, I vomit up my wrong views right away. I have true confidence in the teachings of the Buddha.

Saying this, the king stopped doing bad deeds. He worshipped the Supreme Buddha, got on to his carriage, and headed east towards his kingdom.

4.4 The Ghost Revati

In praise of the lay follower Nandiya's generosity, the Supreme Buddha uttered the following verse.

Supreme Buddha:

When somebody safely returns home having lived in a faraway country for a long time, his relatives, friends, and associates welcome him with joy. In the same way, when someone who does meritorious acts in this world goes to the next world, his own meritorious deeds will welcome him.

Nandiya asked Revati, his wife, to continue practicing generosity when he went away, but Revati stopped. When it was time for her to die, she was addressed by two messengers from hell.

Hell Wardens:

Evil, greedy Revati! Now you must get up. The doors of hell are opening for you. Evil doers have to suffer terribly in hell. We are here to bring you to that miserable world.

Both hell wardens with big red eyes grabbed Revati's hands. They first took her to the Tavatimsa Heaven, where her husband had been reborn.

Revati:

What a wonderful mansion this is! It is made of golden nets, shining like the rays of the sun and filled with beautiful gods. Whose mansion is this? Goddesses with beautiful bodies adorned with sandalwood cream beautify the whole mansion. Who enjoys this heavenly mansion?

Hell Wardens:

In the human world, in the city of Baranasi there was a lay follower named Nandiya who was generous and helpful to others. He is the owner of this beautiful mansion. Goddesses with beautiful bodies adorned with sandalwood cream beautify the whole mansion. Nandiya enjoys this heavenly mansion.

Revati:

Ah! I was Nandiya's wife. I had authority over the whole family. I want to stay and enjoy my husband's mansion. I don't even want to see hell, let alone live there.

Hell Wardens:

Evil woman, the hell for you is down there. You did not do anything to earn merit in the human world. Those who are greedy, make others angry, and lead evil lives can never live with gods.

Revati:

Oh, what is that terrible smell? What is that rotten excrement, urine, and filth?

Hell Wardens:

Evil Revati, this is Samsavaka hell. It is as deep as the height of more than one hundred humans. You are going to boil here for a thousand years.

Revati:

Why? What bad action did I do by body, speech, and mind to have to boil in this terrible hell?

Hell Wardens:

You deceived monks, beggars, and virtuous people with lies. Those were your evil deeds. That is why you have to suffer in this deep hell for a thousand years.

In this hell, beings' hands are cut off, legs are cut off, ears are cut off, and noses are cut off. Then a flock of ravens chase the beings and eat their flesh with their sharp beaks.

Revati:

No, no! Please take me back to the human world. Surely I will do more meritorious deeds. I will practice generosity, behave well, keep the precepts, and restrain my senses. I will do many meritorious deeds which lead to happiness and freedom from remorse.

Hell Wardens:

You are too late. You were heedless in the human world. Now weep! You will experience the results of what you did.

Revati:

Now, when I go back to the human world, who will encourage me to collect merit? Who will ask me to offer robes, shelter, food and drink to virtuous people? Who will teach me that greedy, angry, and evil people won't go to heaven?

Surely when I go from this world to the human world I will practice generosity, behave well, keep the precepts, and restrain the senses. I will do many meritorious deeds.

I will enthusiastically make bridges in places where it is hard to cross, plant trees, set out pots of water for drinking, build parks and ponds. Furthermore, I will observe the Eight Precepts four times a month on each of the four moon phases. I will protect the precepts carefully and practice generosity eagerly. I have seen the results of merit with my own eyes.

Shaken with fear, Revati was deluded in thinking that she could return to the human world. The hell wardens grabbed her legs, turned her upside down and threw her into the terrible Samsavaka Hell.

Revati:

Previously I was very greedy and insulted monks and virtuous people. I cheated on my husband and lied to him. Now I am boiling in this frightful hell.

4.5 Sugar Cane Ghost

Ghost:

Bhante, as a result of my meritorious deeds, a large farm of sugar cane has appeared for me. Unfortunately, I am unable to eat from it. Please tell me why I cannot eat them. Even though I try very hard to pluck out a stalk, I fail every time. Leaves of the sugar cane cut my body and I become very weak and faint. I am suffering very much. Please tell me what bad deed I did in the past.

With a weak body I collapse on the ground. I tremble like a fish thrown to the hot ground. I am crying. Please tell me why this is happening to me.

I am starving, thirsty, and weak. Overcome by extreme thirst, I have never experienced any happiness. Please Bhante, tell me how I can eat the sugar cane.

Monk:

You have done an evil deed when you were in the human world. I will tell you what that is.

One day, you were going somewhere while chewing a sugar cane. Another person came up behind you with the idea that you would share with him. But you did not pay attention to him. Then he begged for a sugar cane saying, "Good sir, please give me some sugar cane." With an angry mind, reluctantly, you passed back a sugar cane without looking at him. That is the karma that you are experiencing now. Therefore, now you should also turn your back to the sugar cane and try to pluck it. Then you will be able to eat as much as you wish. In this way you will be happy and satisfied.

So the ghost turned his back to the sugar cane and plucked it out of the ground. He ate as much as he wished. In this way he became happy and satisfied.

4.6 The Ghost Princes

Supreme Buddha:

There once was a city called Savatti located near the Himalaya Mountain. I have heard that there were two princes who lived in that city. They enjoyed sensual pleasures too much and thought only about happiness in the present life and not the future.

When they died, they were reborn in the ghost world. Experiencing the results of the evil deeds that they did, with invisible bodies, in the same city, they were crying with regret.

Ghost:

Alas, we had plenty of food and wealth. There were also lots of noble monks living in the city. But we did not give anything to them. We did not collect any merits leading to happiness.

Previously, we were the sons of a royal family. But now we are suffering in the ghost world with hunger and thirst. What greater misfortune can there be than this? When we were in the human world, we were rulers, but in the ghost world, we are not. Having fallen from a high status to low, we are suffering. We are roaming for food, overcome by hunger and thirst.

Supreme Buddha:

Too much enjoyment caused this misfortune. Having understood this danger, one should not be intoxicated with pleasures and not be arrogant. That wise person, after death will be reborn in heaven.

4.7 The Son of a King

Supreme Buddha:

That prince experiences all these wonderful things as a result of his previous good karma, but he is obsessed by delightful forms, sounds, smells, tastes, and touches. One day he went to a park and enjoyed dancing, singing, and playing sports. Upon returning, he entered the city of Rajagaha. There, he saw a Pacceka Buddha named Sunetta who was very calm, concentrated, and virtuous. He led a very simple life. He was on his alms round begging for food.

The prince was riding an elephant, so he climbed down and asked the Buddha mockingly, "Bhante, did you get food?" The prince forcefully snatched the Buddha's bowl from his hands and smashed it on the ground. Laughing at the Buddha he said, "Hey monk, I am the son of King Kitava. You cannot do anything to me."

The result of that evil deed was very painful. After death, he fell directly into hell. He suffered for a long time. Exactly how long? Six times eighty-four thousand years. That many years he had to suffer in the miserable hell. One time he was boiled legs first, and another time he was boiled head first.

One time boiled from the left side, another time boiled from the right side. Thus he experienced immense pain.

Having gotten angry at that Buddha who never got angry, the foolish prince suffered many hundreds and thousands of years in hell. After a very long time, he died there and was reborn in the ghost world as a ghost suffering from hunger and thirst.

Arrogance caused this misfortune. Having understood the danger of too much enjoyment, wise people should be very humble. If one respects the Buddhas, that person is praised in this very life. After death, that wise person will be reborn in heaven.

4.8 Excrement Eating Male Ghost

Moggallana Bhante:

Oh unlucky one, you are standing in a pit of excrement. Who are you? What kind of evil deed did you do? How can I know for sure what happened to you?

Ghost:

Bhante, I am a ghost. As a result of my evil deeds I have been born in this ghost world. I am suffering very much

Moggallana Bhante:

What kind of evil deed did you do by body, speech, or mind to suffer like this?

Ghost:

When I was in the human world, I let a monk stay in my house. The monk was very greedy and jealous of his supporters. He insulted good monks.

I listened to that evil monk's words. Following him, I too insulted good monks. That is the evil deed I did from which I was reborn in the ghost world.

Moggallana Bhante:
You associated with that evil monk thinking that he was a good friend. What happened to the monk after death?

Ghost:
Bhante, that evil monk has also been born in the ghost world. He is suffering in the same pit of excrement where I suffer. I am standing on his head. He lives as a servant to me here.

Bhante, I have to eat other people's excrement, while he has to eat mine.

4.9 Excrement Eating Female Ghost

Moggallana Bhante:
Oh unlucky one, you are standing in a pit of excrement. Who are you? What kind of evil deed did you do? How can I know for sure what happened to you?

Ghost:
Bhante I am a ghost. As a result of my evil deeds I have been born in this ghost world. I am suffering very much.

Moggallana Bhante:
What kind of evil deed did you do by body, speech, or mind to suffer like this?

Ghost:

When I was in the human world, I let a monk stay in my house. The monk was very greedy and jealous of his supporters.

I listened to that evil monk's words. Following him, I too insulted good monks. That is the evil deed I did from which I was reborn in the ghost world.

Moggallana Bhante:

You associated with that evil monk thinking that he was a good friend. What happened to the monk after death?

Ghost:

Bhante, that evil monk has also been born in the ghost world. He is suffering in the same pit of excrement where I suffer. I am standing on his head. He lives as a servant to me here.

Bhante, I have to eat other people's excrement, while he has to eat mine.

4.10 Large Group of Ghosts

Moggallana Bhante:

You are naked, very thin, and ugly. Your rib bones are pressing against your skin. Who are you?

Ghost:

Bhante, we are ghosts. When we were in the human world we did evil deeds. After death we were reborn in this ghost world and now suffer very much.

Moggallana Bhante:

What evil did you do by body, speech and mind to have come to this ghost world?

Ghosts:

There were many virtuous people and opportunities for collecting merits but we did not give anything. Now we have been roaming for half a month suffering from thirst.

When we feel very thirsty, we go to the river to drink. When we get close to it, the water appears as if it has dried up and all that is left is dry sand. When we are scorched by the sun, we go to the shade of a tree. Once we get there the shade disappears and the sun beats down.

A wind like fire blows and burns us. But we deserve this because we have done lots of evil deeds in our previous life. We are overcome by hunger. We travel many miles searching for food but we cannot find any. We faint and fall on the ground on our backs. Other times we fall face down. We hit our own heads and chests with frustration. Alas, this is our lack of merit. But we deserve this and other more terrible results than this. When we were rich, we did not give anything to others. We did not collect any merit.

Once we escape from this ghost world and are reborn in the human world we hope that we will be generous and virtuous. We must do many wholesome deeds.

4.11 The Woman from Pataliputta

When a man who was attached to a woman died on an ocean journey, he was reborn as a ghost in that same ocean. He found the woman and brought her to live in the ghost world for a year. Then she asked to be returned to her home.

Ghost:

You have seen hell beings, animals, ghosts, asuras, as well as gods and humans. You have seen how they experience the results of their own karma. Now I am going to take you to Pataliputta city. When you go there, you must do meritorious deeds.

Woman:

Friend, you wish for me to be happy. I will do what you say. Please be my teacher. I have seen hell beings, animals, ghosts, asuras, as well as gods and humans and how they experience the results of their own karma. I must do lots of meritorious deeds.

4.12 The Mango Ghost

A group of traders see a ghost and ask about his beautiful park.

Traders:

This lotus pond of yours is extremely delightful. It has beautiful, even banks; it is full of water; flowers are everywhere, and bees can be heard buzzing all around. How did you gain this beautiful pond?

This mango park of yours is also very beautiful and mangoes grow all year round. The trees are covered in flowers and bees can be heard buzzing everywhere. How did you gain this delightful mango park?

Ghost:

My daughter is in the human world right now. She offered mangos, water, and rice gruel to the Buddha and the monks and shared the merit with me. That is how this pond, Mango Park, and cool shade appeared for me.

Later on the daughter finds out about the result of her merit and tells her son,

Daughter:

Understand the good results of giving, living a life of restraint, and following precepts. I was a servant in my master's family, then I became the daughter-in-law of the same family. Now I have become the mistress of the house. This is all the result of doing good deeds.

4.13 The Axle

When a trader's cart axle broke, a man made a new axle from wood and gave it to him. The man was then reborn as an earth deva as a result of this gift. The earth deva goes to the trader's house and praises giving.

Earth Deva:

The result of giving will not always equal the gift itself. The result that is experienced will always be multiplied. Therefore, one should give gifts frequently. Having practiced generosity, one can get rid of suffering in this life and in the next. As a result of giving, beings are born as humans and gods. Therefore, you should be enthusiastic about doing good deeds. Do not miss this opportunity.

4.14 Accumulation of Wealth

Women traders who made money cheating people were reborn as ghosts. This is how they cried.

Ghosts:

We earned money in good ways and in bad ways. Now our wealth is enjoyed by others. What we have here is only misery.

4.15 Wealthy Sons of Wealthy Merchants

A group of ghosts were feeling guilty for their bad deeds and cried out these verses.

First Ghost:

Sixty thousand years have passed while we have been boiling in hell. When will this suffering end?

Second Ghost:

Dear friends, our suffering seems to last forever. This is the result of evil deeds done by us.

Third Ghost:

We were very evil in the human world. Even though we had lots of money, we did not practice generosity, we did not collect merit.

Fourth Ghost:

Once I escape from this ghost world and am reborn in the human world, I hope that I will be generous and virtuous. I must do many wholesome deeds.

4.16 Hit by Sixty Thousand Hammers

Moggallana Bhante:

Why do you look like a crazy person? Why are you running around like a scared animal? You must have done lots of evil deeds in the past. Why do you make that screeching noise?

Ghost:

Bhante, I am a ghost. As a result of my evil deeds, I am experiencing much suffering. From all directions sixty thousand hammers fly towards me and split my head.

Moggallana Bhante:

What kind of evil deed did you do by body, speech, and mind to have sixty thousand hammers fly towards you from all directions and split your head?

Ghost:

When I was in the human world, I saw a Pacceka Buddha named Sunetta. That fearless Buddha was meditating under a tree. I punched him with my fist and split his head. It is as a result of that deed that I have to suffer like this. From all directions sixty thousand hammers fly towards me and split my head.

Moggallana Bhante:

You deserve to have sixty thousand hammers fly towards you from all directions and split your head. Evil doer, this is happening according to your evil deed.

Mahamegha English Publications:

Sutta Translations

Stories of Sakka, Lords of Gods: Sakka Samyutta
Stories of Brahmas: Brahma Samyutta
Stories of Heavenly Mansions: Vimanavatthu
Stories of Ghosts: Petavatthu
The Voice of Enlightened Monks: The Theragatha
The Voice of Enlightened Nuns: The Therigatha
What does the Buddha really teach? (Dhammapada)
What Happens After Death - Buddha Answers
Pali and English Maha Satipatthana Sutta

Dhamma Books

Mahamevnawa Pali-English Paritta Chanting Book
The Wise Shall Realize
The Life of the Buddha for Children
Buddhism
Kondanna the First Bhikkhu

Children's Picture Books

Chaththa Manawaka
Sumina the Novice Monk
Stingy Kosiya of Town Sakkara
Kisagothami
Kali the She-Devil
Ayuwaddana Kumaraya
Sumana the Florist
Sirigutta and Garahadinna
The Banker Anāthpiṇḍika
Kali the She-Devil
Ayuwaddana Kumaraya
Sumana the Florist
Sirigutta and Garahadinna
The Banker Anāthpiṇḍika

To order, go to www.mahamevnawabm.org